DUPLICITY:
MY MOTHERS'
SECRETS

DUPLICITY: MY MOTHERS' SECRETS

Donna Freed

MUSWELL
PRESS

First published by Muswell Press in 2022
Typeset by M Rules

Extract from *New York Daily News* feature by kind
permission New York Daily News.
Extract from *New York Daily Post* feature by kind
permission New York Daily Post.
Extract from the *New York Times* © 1966 The New York Times
Company. All rights reserved. Used under license.
Extract from *The Baby Tree* by Rosalie Sorrels © Grimes Creek Music Co.
Used by kind permission of Carlin Music Delaware LLC. All rights reserved.

Printed and bound by
CPI Group (UK) Ltd, Croydon CR0 4YY

A CIP catalogue record for this book
is available from the British Library

ISBN: 9781739879433
eISBN: 9781739879440

Muswell Press
London N6 5HQ
www.muswell-press.co.uk

To Ruth and Mira

The thin white envelope contained a single page with a total of three facts:

Age of Mother: 27 years

Nationality of Mother: Swiss

Health History of Birth Mother: There were no children born to your mother prior to you.

About my birth father it merely stated: Not reported.

Swiss? A yodeller? A chocolate-loving banker or watch-maker? How was it possible that I, perennially late, sloppy, disorganised, somewhat wild, was derived from Swiss stock? Hackneyed stereotypes aside, Swiss didn't seem to fit, but Swiss was all I had.

'Not reported' is repeated twenty-six times for ethnic background, height, weight, hair and eye colour, race, skin colour, religion, education, occupation, talents, hobbies and interests. As to the Health History of the Birth Father, 'no information was reported.'

'But Swiss? Really? Me?' I pestered Simon, incredulous.

'It's not so very different from what you thought might be the case: Polish or German, possibly Russian,' my husband pointed out. These were the combined nationalities of my adopted families and my looks echoed that profile in a loose way.

'Is Swiss a bit too dull for you? Doesn't quite fit your fantasy?' he asked, utterly nailing it. I had indeed fantasised about my birth mother, a woman with frizzy hair and an ashtray slung around her neck who lounged about on slip-covered furniture out on Long Island. She didn't seem very Swiss to me.

By the time the social worker from Spence-Chapin got back to me, the school year had begun. My patience was further tested with an exasperating, week's long game of phone tag. Finally, we connected and she apologised for taking so much time to prepare the report. She explained that it had taken her longer than usual, there was a slew of material to sift through in the much larger than expected file.

'Before I take you through it, Donna' she cautioned, 'I need to prepare you for a very dramatic story.'

PART I

My mother Ruth

1

IF YOU DON'T BELIEVE ME (1973)

'You know, we were all adopted.' My sister Leah stands framed in her bedroom doorway, her dark braids covering the fists of her crossed arms. Her tone is matter of fact, blasé even, a simple statement of the obvious. There is no sneering singsong of 'I know something you don't know'; this is a more assured superiority, a bit detached, delivered without preamble, head tilted as she looks down on me. This is Claudius casually pouring poison into the ear of Hamlet's father and then standing back, waiting for the caustic to work its corrosive way through to my heart.

'You were adopted' is one of the classic taunts of childhood; one of the first ways we say, 'you don't belong.' But this was no idle threat.

My tongue sticks to the roof of my mouth with my first intake of breath and I almost choke. Heart slamming, I fix my bulging eyes on the floral, ceramic name-plate glued to my sister's door, determinedly avoiding her gaze.

'If you don't believe me, ask Paul, he's six years older than you and he would remember when they brought you home,' she says, calmly killing off all possible doubt.

'They' were our parents. In one searing cut, I was severed from them. I was no longer theirs and they were no longer mine. I was six years old and the one thing that defined me – that was the most important aspect of my life – was a lie. I was not my parents' child, Mom and Dad were not my parents, so we were not a real family; and 'they' hadn't even bothered to tell me.

I didn't doubt my sister, not for one second. I had no need and no desire to doublecheck with my brother and to ask my parents was unthinkable. The panic flooded in because it felt true, it answered every unformed question and realised every unnamed fear. Unacknowledged suspicions were confirmed and the blow I had secretly expected fell, a tiny kernel of knowledge now unfurling inside me that this had all been too good to be true.

It was 1973 and we lived in White Plains, New York where we had moved from Queens three years earlier. My parents chose the suburban neighbourhood for the schools and paid for the house in cash. Mom and Dad were Ruth and Sy (short for Seymour). He was a civil engineer and she was a home-maker with a doctorate in Psychology. My brother, the eldest, was born in 1961, my sister came along three years later and finally I arrived after another three years in March 1967, seemingly inevitable links in a chain.

My family was my world, my religion, and I exalted the people in it to the status of gods. Granted they were like the gods of ancient Greece: capricious, vengeful and vain, prone to petty rivalries – like teenagers with superpowers – but gods nonetheless and awesome in every aspect, displaying every shade of light and dark. My mother, I revered above all the others; she was Zeus, Athena and The Furies combined.

When I sat snuggled on the bed between my parents, with my siblings on the floor in front, our black and white television flickering before us, I, a mere mortal, was granted a glimpse of the view from Mount Olympus. That status and the safety of being cocooned by my people had now been shattered by Leah's thunderbolt and I was cast out.

Years later, my mother would claim that our adoption was never a secret but it was clear to me that my parents – they – didn't want me to have this vital bit of information. And what is a secret? A secret is something hidden, not meant to be heard, or seen, or known and above all, not to be spoken of. And I was not then in the habit of questioning the gods.

The subject of our adoption had never been uttered, let alone discussed before this moment and it was not raised by me or indeed anyone else in my family for another eight years. By the time I turned twenty-one it had been mentioned on only two occasions.

As well as being secret, it was also clearly shameful in an unnameable way. Adopted, in the way that Leah had said it, sounded bad. She did not whisper it in the way that implied we had some special powers but couldn't tell anyone; it was not joyful and it was certainly not cause for celebration. It changed something fundamental about us so that we were now tarnished and dirty.

If it wasn't shameful, why had no one mentioned it? This was not something inconsequential, beneath consideration or discussion; this was a secret with power, the power to disown and to shame. Once exposed, it branded me with the knowledge, conferring the shame of itself, its deficiency and failure, onto me. The shroud of shame seemed to fit and belong to me in a way I no longer did within my family.

I didn't question this shame. I didn't question where it

came from or whose humiliation I was ingesting. Like so much else, I swallowed it whole.

Shame is my first memory. I was no more than three and slept in the crib in my brother's room in the three-bedroom house, or junior three as it was known, in Queens. There were two small bedrooms, the third, a sliver of a room, was my sister's. I lie on my back in the early morning and my father comes in smiling. He reaches underneath me, 'Wet', he says. I can feel his disappointment. Shame, with a little flare of fear, settles on me like a fine mist. And he walks out.

Memories are tricky and fickle but my mother was surprised at the accuracy and clarity of my memory of that room in the house we left when I was three. I have another early memory from that house which feels so genuine I could lick it. It is my third birthday, and my mother and Nana, my maternal grandmother, are there, sitting at the dining table. Nana is smoking. I am in my highchair. In front of me is a bowl of ice cream with a candle in it, the ice cream is melting, my mother is smiling. I am happy. But this memory comes from a photograph, static and flat in black and white. There are no photographs of my brother's room with my crib in the middle of the floor.

The evidence of our adoption was clear from the moment Leah told me and a certain ambivalence on my mother's part suddenly made sense. A kindergarten homework assignment, a good thirty years before the likes of *Heather Has Two Mommies* penetrated the curriculum, tasked us with determining which of our two parents we most resembled.

'I look more like Daddy because we both have blue eyes and blond hair,' I asserted.

'Okay,' my mother replied with a shrug, in a 'have it your way' dismissal. There was no, 'you have my eyes, but my mother's nose and your dad's ears but my fingers' or 'you're

8

the very image of your grandmother.' Just a shrug. Of course, I didn't know anything was missing, until I did and then the glaring and compounded lies sprang from all sides.

The collusion was so complete that no one else in our family seemed bothered by the knowledge of our adoption or even gave any outward sign of it. In my shock, it didn't occur to me to ask my sister how she knew, when and how she found out. She pointed out that my brother knew and my parents had to know. It was clear to me that Leah wasn't too happy about it but prior to telling me, she had betrayed no sign of it. So they had all known, except me, the youngest, the family dupe.

I didn't look at her in the car later that weekend when my father started singing a family favourite, I just joined in.

> This is the day they give babies away
> With a half a pound of tea.
> You just open the lid, and out pops the kid
> With a twelve month guarantee.
> This is the day they give babies away
> With a half a pound of tea
> If you know any ladies who need any babies
> Just send them round to me . . .

My parents had given me a record player and with it, two second-hand records. One was Pete Seeger and The Weavers singing 'Wimoweh' and the other was a compilation of folk songs from around the world. It had a deep scratch across all but this song by singer-songwriter Rosalie Sorrels (June 24, 1933 – June 11, 2017).

Sorrels terminated her first, out-of-wedlock pregnancy, then gave her next child up for adoption when she became pregnant after a rape. She had five more children with her husband. She introduced the song, 'Baby Rocking Medley,' like so:

'All right, it's 5:30 in the morning. That kid has not quit howling now for six hours. You're getting sort of desperate, breaking out into a cold sweat because you know that all those other kids are going to get up in about another half hour and they're going to demand cereal and peanut sandwiches and milk. And you forgot to get milk. Oh, God. All the paregoric is gone. It's gone because you drank it. Things are getting awful bad and you need something else. Every culture's got one: it's the hostile baby-rocking song. You just can't keep all that stuff bottled up inside yourself. You need to let it out some way, or you'd get strange . . . punch the baby in the mouth . . . and you can't do that. You'd get an awful big ticket for it, and it makes you feel lousy. So you take that baby and you rock it firmly, smile sweetly . . . and you sing the hostile baby-rocking song.'

2

BIRTHDAY PRESENCE
(1973–79)

It is impossible to judge the past by the norms and mores of today, but even by the standards of the 1960s and '70s, my parents made mistakes. Were there mitigating circumstances? Aren't there always? However, different choices could have been made. My mother did not always do 'the best she could', and neither did my father. But I can't know which parts of their parenting felt like choices to them. I didn't question the decisions, I only lived with their consequences.

I was in awe of my family; these giants who surrounded me were both protective and oppressive. They were the boundary that defined the parameters of my world, demarcating outside and inside. I knew to be wary of outsiders, but inside the perimeter I was defenceless. When I opened my eyes in my life, my parents and siblings were already there, unquestionable in their prior arrival and authority.

I walked into an established hierarchy of rules, an insidious game with escalating challenges and repercussions, a snakes-and-ladders landscape littered with invisible obstacles. I struggled to navigate the Byzantine complexities.

I don't know whether I accepted these rules and my parents' utter authority because I was the youngest or just because I was a kid. Later on, I would wonder about the nature and origin of this acquiescence. I don't know if this passivity was sewn into me or onto me. I do know that I was predisposed to be amenable to my family's wishes above my own. The love and attention I craved were directly delivered, or so I believed, by slavishly complying to the letter of their laws.

My parents were scythed away from me in one slice that day in front of my sister's door. My parents standing as deities in my life only grew as they became more distant. That they held the power to add or subtract me and that this information was withheld from me only proved their omniscience. Knowing I was adopted didn't mean I didn't belong to these people, and I tried in earnest to belong.

Rule number one was: obey my mother in all things regardless of whether they were nonsensical and counter-intuitive. Whether instructions made sense was secondary, compliance was paramount. Don't think, do!

By age six, I had accumulated a small collection of beloved stuffed animals. There was Lovey Bear, a long-legged 'bear' whose canvas limbs were printed with bubbly '60s slogans of love and peace. There was Ducky Donna, a lemony-yellow knitted, squashy bundle with yarn hair, felt beak and feet and 'Donna' sewn onto a heart-shaped badge on her breast; there was Raggedy Ann and Raggedy Andy and Bunny, a faded pastel hand-me-down that I loved for being small and portable. There was a blue walrus that I had inexpertly stitched together and embroidered. Holly was also there, but she sat on my bedside table. She was a replica of Ling-Ling, one of the Smithsonian's National Zoo's giant pandas. Although I adored her, she was made of faux velvet-covered plastic, hard and not bed-friendly.

Each night, I would carefully arrange Ducky Donna, the Raggedys, Walrus and Bunny around my pillow on the corner of my bed that was against the walls. I tucked Lovey in alongside me and then the tea party could begin. Tea was served by the baker who lived on my ceiling. Tea and cakes would be lowered down via a dumbwaiter by the baker and shared out to each guest in turn. I would take mine last and thank the baker. It was with this imaginary artisan baker that I shared my first kiss.

My after-school routine was to go into the kitchen for 'snack' directly upon coming home. Snack was almost invariably apple juice and graham crackers which sometimes had spider eggs on them. I instinctively brushed away the webbed crumbs. A clear rule was to never call attention to my mother's housekeeping in any way. You ate what you were given without complaint, ignoring any added ingredients, whether it was Mom's hair, mould or spider eggs. Don't think, choke it down!

On this day, I skipped home through fallen leaves to find the Formica kitchen table hidden under piled-up packages of rice and pasta. Penne and elbow macaroni cascaded down, slipping on rills of rice, valleys of bow-ties, pasta cushions all leaking their stuffing. Beneath them, snaked a river of blue-and-white-wrapped Ivory soap.

My 'New England thrifty' mother bought in bulk when things were on sale. She was a 'prepper' long before preparing for the apocalypse was a thing, even before it was called hoarding.

'What do you have to say about all this?' Her arms took in the scope of the display.

Eager as ever to please, I tried to glean what was required

of me. Was this a game? Which one doesn't belong? That's too easy, it's obviously the soap. I stood there blank, waiting for a hint.

She reached into the pile and pulled out a bar of the soap which looked as if it had been raked by claws, furrows made in the waxy wrapping, the white soap curled into crusty waves.

'Doesn't it look like little teeth did that?' she asked, her voice almost reasonable.

'Yes! Yes it does look like little teeth did that,' I answered with relief. The mystery was solved and I looked with fresh eyes at the pile of rice and pasta and it became clear, all the bags had been nibbled by little teeth. Aha! We have mice!

However true, it was still the wrong answer. The injunction against noticing the deficiencies in my mother's housekeeping extended to herself. To solve a problem like mice would require outside intervention – the buying of mouse traps at the very least which, as she didn't drive, would involve my father and a hardware store – and therefore acknowledgement of the mice. A better solution to the evidence of mice was to find a different cause.

So, my mother concluded that it was my little teeth that had done the nibbling and scraping of soap and my agreement was a clear and irrefutable admission of guilt. As punishment – do not eat food, whether raw, cooked or indeed soap, that was not specifically allotted to you was a hard and fast rule – all my stuffed animals were taken away and put in the attic the following morning after a final, prolonged tea party and one last lingering kiss from the baker – the end of our brief affair.

When my son Dexter's own collection of cuddly toys threatens to overtake our apartment, I start flailing around with them, 'Why do you want to keep them? You don't even play with them!' I yell.

'Sorry,' I say to Dexter when we're having dinner that evening, 'We'll find a place for all your toys, don't worry, we don't have to give them away. It's just, I used to really play with my stuffed animals . . .'

'I know,' he interrupts, rolling his eyes, 'you used to kiss the baker on the ceiling.'

'I have told you that story. Well, then they all got taken away,' I blurt, my eyes on my plate.

His head whips to mine, 'what did you do?' he asks after a long moment of staring at me.

'We had mice, but my mom blamed me instead and that was my punishment,' I explain in the same even voice I use to explain why he has to go to school or eat fruit or put on his shoes or countless other unwelcome but immutable truths.

'I'm sorry, sweetie, I know that's a bit heavy but I'm telling you because I don't always know the right thing to do. I didn't always have the best example.'

Without a sound, he gently picks up my fork and starts feeding me from my plate. I swallow his spooned up love past the tears that choke my throat.

I don't tell him that my mother took them from the attic and moved them to North Carolina, where my parents retired in 1999 and dotted them around their bedroom. Mementos of my childhood passed up a generation, instead of down. The internal heirlooms that were passed down are larger, less tangible and far less cuddly.

With the word 'adopted,' my identity as my parents' child tilted away from me like a rock detaching from a cliff; but in the vacuum left by my parents, a new alliance and affiliation with my siblings was born. We were tarred with that same brush of 'adopted', lumped together as the us against the parental them. I immediately grasped that we were not biological siblings, but we were all in the same boat and we were bonded with stronger stuff than mere biology: secrecy and collusion.

My sister, while still one of the exalted, was closest to me in both age and inclination. It wasn't exactly an alliance of equals, more like handler and agent. And while it did feel disloyal to turn my allegiance from my mother to my sister, had my mother not betrayed me first?

In John le Carré novels, George Smiley is a masterful handler; the spies in his webs are unwittingly entrapped into betraying their country, their loyalty in turn then welded to him. And how does Smiley do this? Why does it work? Because he too has been betrayed, the same crime perpetrated against him, and he has contorted his hurt into the same shape, love and loyalty inverted. My sister was a master handler and I, a natural born spy.

My free will was subsumed by the dictates of my mother's but submitting to the will of others was also against the rules. Listen to me: think for yourself!

My mother decried my willingness to let other people hold sway over my actions and personality. In particular, my slavish adoration of my sister was problematic. If my big sister Leah did it, I did it. If Leah told me to do it, I did it. If Leah dared me to say it, I said it. My mother started calling me 'Little "Me Too."' 'If your sister jumped off the Brooklyn Bridge would you jump too?'

Thinking for myself was an endless game of chance, trying to land on what won approval and not punishment. I had to weigh my mother's erratic attentions against the conspiratorial camaraderie with my sister. My mother and sister were at either end of the tightrope I trod through childhood.

All this hyper-vigilance was nerve-wracking stuff and I started biting my nails. The sight of my chewed fingers disgusted my mother on an aesthetic level but also the physical evidence of my nervous state unnerved her. 'You have such pretty hands,' she tried cajoling.

When flattery failed, she decreed that I should wear plasters on all ten fingers to school. A girl in my class who also bit her nails applied a foul-tasting solution to repel the biting – Antabuse for nail-biters – but needless to say, my mother didn't entertain that kind of expensive gimmickry. I baulked at the insufferable embarrassment and indignity of the plasters.

It was enough that I wore my brother's hand-me-down Y-front underwear with the hole sewn shut; it was enough that I took my lunch to school in the plastic lining of a cereal box (and when I got an actual brown paper bag, I folded it up and reused it until it disintegrated); it was enough that those lunches consisted of scrambled egg sandwiches that congealed into a cold, eggy sponge-blob by lunch time; it was enough that I looked like a plucked chicken from the home haircuts; it was enough that I wore the same clothes in the class photo for three years running which we got on sale at the thrift store in the first place; it was enough that our house still sported the decals, years later, from the one time we had Halloween decorations because they came free with the newspaper; it was enough that my white tights were discoloured, lumpen with varicose-veins of black, Frankenstein-sutures where they had run and my mother had sewn them. But it was a step too far to expect me to parade through the third grade with plasters on my fingers!

Leah came to the rescue. At the last minute before going to school, she advised, I should run up to 'the children's bathroom' to use the toilet, peel the plasters off and tuck them under a facecloth placed casually on the radiator for this purpose, and then run out to school. At that time Mom was working, so Paul had the key to the basement to let us in the house after school. I should again pretend I had to go to the bathroom, clutching myself and hopping up and down with urgency so he couldn't see my hands and scoot up to the bathroom and jam the plasters back on. This scheme was abandoned when my hands were still bitten raw after a week.

In the escalating stakes, my mother upped the ante, she saw my bandage avoidance and raised me the celebration of my upcoming birthday. It was a shocking and demoralising threat. Each night, as I caught a nail in my teeth, I would tell myself it would be the last one, but I was back at it the next day.

As my birthday approached, it seemed impossible that my nails could grow in time and so, finger in mouth, I resigned myself to not having a birthday. On our birthdays, we got to pick where we got take-out from and there was cake and ice cream. I invariably picked pizza, the thick and pillowy Sicilian style we favoured from the lovely Italian man in Hartsdale who gave me cheese (not soap or rice) to nibble on while we waited for our order. I meekly accepted birthday defeat, chewing my cuticles and comforting myself with remembrances of pizzas past. My brother and sister, however, were outraged and mutinous on my behalf.

They weren't going to capitulate so easily, because if my birthday could be cancelled, any birthday could be cancelled. So my sister propped me up against the wall behind my brother's bed and while she sat twisting the skin of my upper arm on one side, my brother dug under my nails to reveal some white on the other. The searing pain from the pinch was supposed to distract me from the gouging of my nails. 'This is what Indians do,' she explained. The outcome be damned, being wedged between Leah and Paul as they worked to earn me a birthday celebration was better than any pizza.

'Don't bother,' my mother said when she saw us, 'she's not having a birthday.'

When Paul left for college, we still had the key to the basement but we were no longer entrusted with the run of the house after school. My father installed a chain lock across the door that led from the basement to the ground floor. What they failed to appreciate was that along with the laundry room, ping pong table, my father's treadmill and my mother's old psychology textbooks – and no, there was not a bathroom in the place where we were locked for several hours each day – were all of my father's tools. The same key that opened the basement door from the garage, also unlocked the door from the basement to the upstairs. We unlocked the door, unscrewed the bolt and screwed ourselves back in again around the time Mom was due home. We listened to the radio, stole food – or snacked, if you were other people – and watched the fish or the black and white TV that had now moved to a corner of the dining room. There were a couple of heart-poundingly close calls when we were rethreading the screws and locking the door as Mom was opening the front door. One of those days was December 8, 1980 when we heard on the radio that John Lennon had been shot and killed. By the time the soap operas I was watching were interrupted to announce the attempted assassination of Ronald Reagan, on March 30, 1981, my sister had been shipped off to boarding school and I was on my own.

Who had time to fantasise about who my 'real' parents might be when every day was a minefield? But finding out about our adoption seemed to be the catalyst for a type of identity crisis within me. I couldn't see myself. The foundations of my personality, like a cloth whipped away from a table leaving strewn and broken crockery, were obliterated in that one blow.

19

There is a scene in *Duck Soup*, Chico pretends to be Groucho, who has just exited the room. Mrs. Teasdale protests, 'but I saw you with my own eyes!'

Chico says, 'who you gonna believe: me or your own eyes?'

To me, my mother was Chico. She was the last word on everything in our house and clearly knew more about me than I did.

'Am I a happy person?' I asked in the car one day. 'It's hard to tell,' she replied, 'you're like a tropical storm, sunny one minute and dark the next.' Which while it sounded exotic, didn't sound that great.

Another night we were playing checkers on her bed. Checkers was a high-stakes game. When we had gerbils visit our first-grade classroom, Miss Pettymare held up the female and pointed out the nipples running down her belly, 'these are the mammary glands,' she informed us. During checkers with my mother that night, I lifted up my shirt and pointed to my own nipples and said proudly, 'these are my mammary glands!' I was promptly sent to bed.

But this night, I was in sixth grade, around eleven years old. Mom sat cross-legged, pouring over the checkers board in concentration; I knelt on the floor at the end of the bed. My brother was making a racket practising his violin in the full-length mirror in the hallway. 'I have a question to ask you,' I said. She nodded her acquiescence. 'It's important, can I close the door?'

She spread her hands with a big sigh but the roll of her eyes signified a sudden wariness. Her arms said, 'be my guest', the sigh and her eyes added the unsaid 'if you must.' As I crossed to close the door, a flash of inspiration and instantaneous, heady power flooded through me as I understood that she was afraid I was going to ask about our adoption. I savoured her discomfort but, I already knew the answer to that question and I had far more important matters weighing on my mind. I shut the door and turned to square myself off in front of my mother.

'Am I mature enough for my age?' I asked.

Her hands, which had been gripped at her elbows, started waving around. Relief and wonder mixed in her voice, 'Well, Donna,' she said, 'yes and no.'

In P.D. Eastman's 1960 book, *Are You My Mother*, a little bird looks for his mother, never having seen her, he doesn't know what she looks like. He asks a kitten, hen, dog, cow, car, boat, plane and backhoe the same question: 'Are you my mother?' Instead, I seemed to be asking, 'Can you see me?' 'Are you my mirror?'

One of our family myths was that my mother was a child psychologist but in truth she merely *studied* child psychology; she didn't *practise* it. When later on she became overwhelmed and subsumed by doubts and anger, her depression gaining traction, I think her knowledge hindered her parenting more than it helped.

I think she hoped I'd notice only the positive aspects of her mothering and ignore what she preferred not to examine herself. The fact that I'm scary shouldn't cow you. Don't dare defy me but stand up to other people. This was a parenting technique that I squirrelled away for later use and could be summarised by my father's oft repeated: 'do as I say, not as I do.'

My mother would have been familiar with Anna Freud's pioneering work in child psychoanalysis and Kanner's theory of 'refrigerator mothers'. 'Trust yourself. You know more than you think you do,' advised paediatrician of the day, Dr. Spock. She would have read about the importance of attachment and play. It must have filled her with dread when she slipped. How do you trust yourself then?

With knowledge comes power but also tremendous guilt. 'No medical intervention!' was drilled into Simon and me at the natural childbirth classes we attended each week of my pregnancy. If you were weak and allowed the doctors near you, the bond with your child would be interrupted and your child's life chances ruined. My mother was spared that form of guilt but she had a taste of it even earlier when pregnancy didn't come along at all.

As well as the added pressure of knowledge there must have been some in-creep of imposter syndrome. Your right to bear children is unimpeded until it doesn't come naturally. If you persist in your desire for children, you enter the public domain. You open the door to medical experts and social workers to measure and weigh your fitness, examine and chart your progress. Adoption as some version of FILTH in British banking circles: Failed In London, Try Hong Kong. Failed in natural childbearing, try adoption, the latter always thought of as the lesser option and achievement.

These though, were the dark times, made darker still because of the light. And there was light. Perhaps it is the light that helps to normalise and rationalise the dark. I still don't know.

Our house was a place of rituals. Sunday mornings started with blaring classical music and bagels and lox, followed by a family outing. On rainy days we would venture into the city to the Natural History Museum or the Metropolitan Museum of Art, where my mother, ignoring the suggested donation for entry, would hand over a quarter for the five of us. In good weather we walked the nature trails at Cranberry Lake or the Mianus River Gorge, looking for mica and rose quartz. In the autumn there was apple picking or just a visit to the orchard to collect bushels of crisp Macoun apples. We stood at the end of the conveyor belt where the freshly fried doughnuts bobbed along, licking the hot sugar off our fingers and guzzling the thick cider.

We started going to the opera once a year when I was in the fourth grade. *The Marriage of Figaro* was our first. Dad got the tickets from work and the seats were in rows M and N in the orchestra. My father checked out the recording from the library and we listened to a little each night, following along with the libretto. On the day of the opera, I went to work with my mother whose office was in the World Trade Center, Tower One at the time. She took me for lunch at the staff cafeteria near the top and we shared fries. At her prompting, I read my mother the synopsis before each act although we knew it inside and out. We gasped in unison as the star-like chandeliers ascended to the ceiling in the darkening hall.

Middle-class Jewish families in the 1960s and '70s lived as if it were the 1950s and mothers had an evening of rest on Sunday. And yes, we were actually middle-class, not that we knew it with all my mother's obsessive scrimping and saving. My father was in charge of dinner those nights and his culinary repertoire was limited to what he could char in the fireplace. He grilled steaks, which we were allowed to flavour with exactly three drops of Lea & Perrins, and buried potatoes and onions wrapped in foil in the coals. Dessert was either chestnuts or popcorn shaken over the flames. My sister and I saved the Sunday comics to read in front of the fire while my mother languished in a long bath.

My father was smart and silly and fair, fair-haired and fair-minded and he still talked to you when you were in trouble. He marked the Winter Solstice by donning his long johns and an orange ski mask, careering down the hall singing the baseline of the Batman theme, 'duh, nuh, nuh, nuh, nuh, nuh nuh, nuh' and landing in front of you in a spindly-legged cat leap: 'Thermal Man!'

During the working week, I didn't see much of him but I milked my time at bedtime when he tucked me in. Just as he was about to kiss me goodnight, I would ask 'Can I have a glass of water?' I had to sit up to drink the water and so I had to be re-tucked. Of course, then I had to use the toilet earning me a third and final tuck.

I craved and savoured time alone with my mother. I used to do my homework at the kitchen table, both of us toiling away to *All Things Considered* on the radio. Everyone else in the family called me Peach Fuzz due to my lack of hair until I was two, except Mom because she knew I didn't like it. She taught me the song flute and recorder and made me French flash cards. She would play my favourite song on the recorder, the 'Habanera' from *Carmen* while I pranced and cavorted through the upstairs hallway. One afternoon I rushed home to tell my mother that this huge surge of joy had started in my belly and suffused my chest and was beaming up my throat. I felt that same bursting warmth when she would take both my cheeks in her hands and say 'Shnookums!' into my face, squeezing so hard it ached.

And life was always lighter when Uncle Lew, Mom's brother, flew in from his far-flung adventures in Cairo and Paris. My mother's emotional storm-clouds were temporarily dispersed, replaced by the plumes of Lew's cigarette smoke billowing out over the sofa. He brought glamour and exoticism but most importantly of all, he brought laughter.

Once when it was the hour of his departure, my sister and I spontaneously jumped either side of him and tugged him back away from the door. 'Don't go,' we pleaded. Egged on by Lew's giggles, we pressed on. Mom started laughing and in the ensuing contagion, we all abandoned ourselves to the hilarity, the four of us doubled over, sister and brother and sister and sister, in silent, gut-wrenching laughter.

3

THE CAT IS OUT OF THE BAG
(1981–90)

My brother and I are sitting on the kerb outside our house. It's a humid summer night; I'm fourteen, he's twenty and home from university.

'So, were we adopted?' I asked. 'Leah always told me I should ask you, that you would remember because you were six.'

'Of course we were adopted,' he says, with some of that same scornful superiority that Leah had when she told me. 'I remember when you were brought home. Mom had to go somewhere each evening for a week and Dad took Leah and me out for Flying Saucers at Carvel every night. We were so disappointed when they brought you home.' He grins, his face open and lovely and I know he's kidding, as I'm also aware that tucked inside his violin case there is a picture of what must be our first meeting. My mother, looking both bemused and exhausted – standard for all pictures from our youth – is proffering a bald and squalling me while my brother and sister look on, nonplussed.

I don't know what prompted me to ask him at that moment. At fourteen I had been the only child in the house for six months and would be starting high school in the autumn. I had asserted my independence as far as my hair was concerned and finally grown it beyond the crew cut my mother reduced my curly hair to with regular mowings. But because of the singular quality of my now full head of springy, corkscrew curls, I was frequently asked if anyone else in my family had curly hair. Perhaps I had a feeling that it was time to get corroboration of our adoption. Maybe it was a step towards claiming my own identity. It also seemed like grown-up knowledge, and asking about it was a way to appear more mature to my sophisticated, older brother.

When our parents told him he was adopted, Paul said that night, he heard 'chosen' and therefore special and had swanned all over school bragging about it until he was asked to tone down his enthusiastic 'chosen one' rhetoric.

And so, I confirmed my sister's story from eight years before and that seemed to suffice for the next four years.

My earliest memories are characterised by complete thoughts and observations of the world around me, but the advent of puberty and high school spelled a time when I purely felt. I did not reflect, I did not think through other people's perspectives, I did not see that other vantage points existed. This was the first time I felt driven by desire. I was a purely carnal, borderline feral, teenage being.

My sister's abrupt removal to boarding school the year before disturbed the uneasy balance of household power. I was now the sole focus of my parents' attention and control, something I had previously craved but now bitterly resented. Not only was it unwelcome to my now more secretive nature, but it had come at the cost of my sister's banishment. Leah had been my ally, compatriot and in part protectress – she was a lightning rod for Mom's anger and I could always rely on her to be in deeper hot water than me.

If I had been an open book to my mother up to that point, I was more opaque now, obscured by a cloud of hormones and surly attitude. While there remained the excellent student, there was now also the embryonic libertine, the cigarette smoker and imbiber of beer.

My mother responded to these natural developments as she did any other ordinary inconvenience that comes with child-rearing – like getting sick or injured, losing things, breaking things, forgetting things – with Draconian measures. She threatened to send me to a special needs school because of what she perceived as my 'social problems'. She didn't like my friends, 'I don't think she's a good influence on you,' was a frequent refrain. I found this continuation of the theme that I was a follower – 'Little Me-Too' all over again – insulting, infuriating and alienating.

While I was far too cowardly to pull some of the stunts that my more daring and possibly more desperate sister per-petrated, I was still treated as though I had or was just about to. My mother didn't see me, she saw me as a me-too, my potential to replicate my sister's behaviour. If I was going to be treated like a juvenile delinquent, I thought, I may as well avail myself of some of the rewards of the crimes.

And so, I stole lipstick and candied peanuts from Woolworths, I skipped school and snuck out of the house at night, pinched six packs of Dad's beer, I tried pot and once, cocaine. My parents were aware of only a fraction of my carryings-on but took a whack-a-mole approach to what they did find out. I was grounded from November 1982 until June 1983. Other than my regular Friday night babysitting gig, I was allowed to walk the three miles home from school with friends and I was permitted to meet a friend on weekend afternoons. I was grounded because instead of going running – which I did most mornings – I got up early and went to a friend's house to watch the sunrise. When I didn't return after my run, my father called the police. When the vice principal called Mom after I had talked back to a teacher, she didn't speak to me for three months; barely civil, she would hurl toast onto the table in front of me at breakfast.

In the midst of all this flux and antagonism, I developed an eating disorder which even at that time I was able to understand was an attempt to have control over something in my life, my body. What started as anorexia blossomed into a bout of bulimia.

With hindsight, I see that it must have been frightening for my parents, that it was desperately hard to reach me. I bristled with the bravado and fragility of a teenager. I wore an impervious shield of rejection against my mother. While I hurtled along, a storm of emotion and reaction, my mother saw me on a precipice, that I might tumble over the edge. She saw me as a runaway truck, stripped of its brakes and unable to control the monsters and messes of my own making.

When I look back now, I believe my mother suffered from depression, but I don't know that for a fact because, to my knowledge, it was never diagnosed or treated. She never discussed it with me either at that time or any time afterwards. I used to sum it up with 'my mother spent ten years in bed.' Around the time of my sixth birthday, which also happened to be when I found out that we were adopted, it seemed like a red mist descended upon her, flattening her to her bed nearly all the time, roused only by routine or anger.

I suspect it was a gradual silting up from a rising tide of feeling overwhelmed which she tried to tamp down through a total intolerance of disobedience, ratcheting up the rules in order to maintain her illusion of control. By the time I first noticed, it had built to a crescendo and had fully taken over.

I think I conflated the two things (her depression and the adoption revelation) as concurrent because that revelation was the first time I was jolted out of my complacent acceptance of all things familial. It has to be said that there were signs that all was not well. There were the intractable and unbreakable rules and the fact that it was inconceivable that I would approach my parents with the knowledge of our adoption without them having mentioned it first. From my perspective, our household felt scary and unpredictable.

Equally, I have no idea what awakened in my mother to bring her out of her malaise, only that she awoke. Whether it was an act of will or simply the passage of time, I cannot say. But when I was at my teenaged worse, she changed. She stopped viewing me as a potential problem and started trying to figure out who I was. She leaned all the way over to me, to listen, to listen with her whole body. It was, on the surface, a subtle shift but represented a radical sea change.

The atmosphere in our house went from dangerous to neutral, one of comparative safety and acceptance, like the blaring silence after an alarm has stopped ringing. We went from a near-capsizing boat to a merely rocking one.

It took some time but under that unfamiliar – and initially not only uncomfortable but unwelcome – attention, I eventually turned to her like a flower to the sun. I was wary, I still hid what I thought was undesirable, unlovable, unforgivable; I didn't trust this newfound focus. But I grew bolder with my mother as she softened to me.

However, her temper reignited in the face of my academic senior year slump when a lone 'C' landed on my report card for the first time. 'Things are going to change around here,' was my mother's parting shot as I left the house for school the following morning.

When I came back after school, Mom was sitting at the kitchen table. 'Sit,' she gestured to what was still my assigned seat. She nudged at a letter that was on the corner of the table. My pulse quickened when I saw it was from Vassar College. I stuck my thumb into the thick envelope and roughly tore it open. I took the single sheet of paper out slowly and deliberately unfolded it.

'I got in!'

At which happy news my mother erupted. 'If you think I'm going to pay for you to do the bare minimum at Vassar, you can think again. You can go to a state school!' she bellowed.

I don't remember what I yelled back but Vassar College was my holy grail; this was my bus ticket out of town. I was so certain that I wanted Vassar that I didn't even bother to complete my application to Wellesley College, my mother's alma mater, which was just as prestigious and I stood a very good chance of getting in as an alum's daughter. At my Vassar interview, I bombarded the interviewer with more questions than he asked me. I was going to Vassar College come what may!

We proceeded to yell back and forth until I burst into angry tears, accusing her of spitefully taking away the one thing I wanted for one C! Why did she hate me so? And then she started crying, a sight I had never seen before, a sight that illuminated my mother's earnest concern. We looked at each other through our tears and then we started talking. I sat close to her on the bed and we hugged, happiness and celebration flooding back. I got in!

And then my mother said, 'Donna, I hope you take what I say and really think about it. Don't just reject it because it's me who said it. But think about it and see if it works for you.

I haven't done much actual doing in my life but I've done a lot of thinking.' She set me free.

Bemused at the change in atmosphere from the morning, my father took us out to dinner that night. 'I don't understand how I could feel so angry and sad and then so happy,' I said.

'It's called catharsis,' Mom said, with a smile.

National Honor Society Induction took place a few weeks before graduation; it was a proud evening event when our names would be called out for awards and scholarships. A friend from my field hockey team and I toasted our cleverness over a couple of White Russians that afternoon before the ceremony: 'White Russians! We're committing genocide!' Our optimism and assurance about our promising futures beaming out of us in the dark bar.

Filled with Dutch (or White Russian?) courage, I found my mother in the kitchen, preparing dinner.

'I have some questions,' I launched at her. Once again, the 'hey ho, here we go' sigh and shrug to arm herself against whatever might follow. 'Okay,' she said.

'Was I adopted?'

She stopped chopping and looked at me evenly, 'I know you know you were adopted through channels in the family.'

If this makes us sound like the Corleones of The Godfather, there's a reason. Perhaps a more apt comparison would be the Gambino crime family. This was 1985, the year John Gotti murdered Paul Castellano, head of the Gambino crime family outside of Sparks Steak House on East 46th Street. My father worked in New York City construction, which was controlled by the Mafia. If they wanted to shut down your job, it was shut. And so when I went to work with him, he would point out the gentlemen in the trailer who were there to clock in and out and collect a pay-check, but do nothing else. Our family wasn't so different; we were secretive, prone

31

to retaliation and biblical punishments. 'Channels in the family' evoked the various alliances and ties between our different factions, the shifting loyalties and side deals. It also meant there was a rat. I immediately thought back to that steamy evening four years earlier, outside on the kerb with my brother. Enough said, see if I confided in him again. The old grooves and grievances of our childhood once again reared their tired heads.

Clearly, I had been the more mature of the two of us that night; while I had been satisfied with the confirmation and extra information, he had seen fit to play tattletale and run to Mommy to tell her I had asked if we were adopted. Who else could it have been?

'Okay, so why were we adopted?' I brazenly pressed on.

Her face blushed a blotchy red and she hunched back over the table.

'There were conception problems; that's why you were adopted,' she whispered to the table.

Her wound broke open and her shame, tangible and mal-odorous, billowed up and mushroomed above us.

This really was grown-up information and whatever my reaction was to finally hearing her say that I was adopted, it was overshadowed by her already knowing that I knew and then lost in the broader context of a story that began with her pain.

It's hard to say where family stories begin, what grains of truth their woolly contours contain. Because I was the youngest, the origins of events that transpired before I was born were unverifiable hearsay. The five of us had different perspectives born of our ages and position. Some of these assigned roles were fixed throughout life, some fluid enough to evolve in adulthood. But there was a lot of 'before you were born' time when some stories had already solidified.

After this conversation with my mother, such as it was, I formed the notion that the reason my parents didn't tell me I was adopted was that Paul had been a braggart, as he had admitted in our one adoption discussion, and Leah had taken it badly. I don't know where I got that idea, I have a vague recollection of Leah telling me that in her room one day but nothing more. It was an idea that seemed to blossom out of nowhere, a composite of the same hazy connections and partial truths that family lore and conspiracy theories are made of.

How these two minuscule bits of information ('I know you knew' and that their inability to conceive was a matter of shame) concreted into this adoption-creation myth is difficult to say. Each time the adoption was raised – and this was the third occasion – another tiny chunk of information was loosed.

Another humid scorcher fifteen years after Leah's initial divulgence, seven after my conversation with Paul and three after the brief interview with Mom; I was twenty-one. We sprawled on the back deck, the crickets chirping around us. Leah, Paul and I were all home, a rare occurrence.

At last, I too was an adult; I had crossed an invisible threshold. The first time Paul called me my freshman year of college, I heard it in his voice. He addressed me as an equal, or if not an equal, close enough. 'Are you talking to me differently because I'm out of the house?' I asked. 'Yes,' he admitted with a laugh.

'When were they going to tell me I was adopted?' I complained. 'They told you and you were so excited to have been chosen you blabbed about it to everyone and you were told to simmer down about it,' I said to my brother.

I turned to Leah, 'when they told you, you were so angry it started a war between you and Mom and so they decided not to tell me.'

'They never told me,' my sister said into the night. 'I found out at the optometrist's; I was getting my eyes tested and the doctor asked if astigmatism ran in the family and Dad answered, "I don't know, the kids were all adopted."'

This is not my personal memory but after that, I always imagined my sister with her grave face, framed by her long, dark braids, pressed up against the phoropter in the darkened room, the hypnotic swish of the flicked lenses. 'Which is better, this one – *swish . . .click* – or this one – *swish . . .click*?' Did she feel like she was eavesdropping on her own life? Did she feel trusted with a big secret? Burdened by it? Did she feel forgotten and overlooked and that the secret had merely slipped out because Dad forgot she was in the room? That she wouldn't know what was being said? Did she feel honoured and anointed by the knowledge, deemed grown up enough to be told? That it was Dad's way of sharing the secret with her?

I had asked when they were going to tell me but the point was academic. I did know, and as my mother asserted, she knew I knew. But what I didn't know was how long she had known that I knew.

That night was the first time that I would hear the name Barbara Miller and extremely uncharacteristically, I would need reminding of it numerous times. But I always remembered what she told my brother.

While still at university, Paul decided he wanted to find his biological mother and so he made an appointment with one Barbara Miller, a senior social worker and head of the Post-Adoption Service at the Louise Wise Agency in Manhattan through whom we were all adopted.

By his own account, he swaggered into her office, plunked down a bottle of Courvoisier and propped his feet up on her desk. Leaning back in his chair, arms folded, he announced, 'I want to find my mother.'

In my mind's eye, I see Barbara, her eyes sliding from my brother's face, settling with pronounced distaste on his feet; she ignores the inexplicable and uncouth bottle of brandy. Before she speaks, a hand goes to the pearls around her peter-pan-collared neck. She sits erect and prim, her grey hair in a pristine bun, pinned against her head, eyes enormous behind her glasses. At last, having gathered herself, she fixes him with a withering gaze and states, 'You are only looking for this woman because you want a distraction from other problems in your life. If that woman had wanted to know you, then she would have kept you.'

Later on, the lawsuits, the articles, the film *Three Identical Strangers* (2018) would reveal that this practised, blanket dismissal of adopted children was the very least of Barbara Miller's and the Louise Wise Agency's many crimes and misdemeanours.

Back on the deck, Paul casually added, 'Mom told me not to tell you I was looking for my mother at the time because you were having a hard enough time as it was.'

I flushed hot with retrospective adolescent anger at having been thought incapable of coping with this information, underestimated yet again.

Still, I somehow felt bolstered by this revelation. It was clear that conversation around this topic was possible with my mother. It really was high time I addressed the issue head-on with Mom and we were, by this time, quite close.

For adoption-conversation number two with my mother, we were predictably in the kitchen and I again began without preamble:

'Why didn't we ever talk about us being adopted?'

'It was never a secret,' she said, defensiveness making her stand a little taller.

'We never talked about it. When I asked you about it when I was eighteen, you said you knew that I knew ...'

' . . .through channels in the family,' we said in unison.

'I know,' she said.

'So I figured that Paul must have told you after I asked him but actually Leah told me when I was six.'

'I know. She came and told me right after she told you.'

My mother's words rocked through me. I was catapulted right back to that day, standing speechless outside my sister's door. The sensation of the floor dropping, my foundations giving way, my perception of the world disintegrating.

'So you knew I knew when I was six and you didn't talk to me about it?'

'I figured the cat was out of the bag and if you had any problems with it, you would come to me.'

When we were kids, my sister and I would pick dandelions, grasp them in our fists and flick the heads off with our thumbs, the yellow flower tops reeling away, while chanting, 'my mamma had a baby and its head popped off.' That was me, my head popped off.

I gaped, goggle-eyed at my mother who stood there composed and a little bemused at my stunned reaction.

So at the wise old age of six, it was my responsibility to come forward with any 'issues' I might have had with my entire universe crumbling to pieces but at seventeen I was evidently too delicate and fragile to be told that my brother was looking for his biological mother?

Even George Bush Jr knew that you have to 'control the message!'. When my sister waltzed up to my mother and announced, 'I just told Donna we were adopted,' did she not think that Leah might have put a negative spin on that little story? That how you hear something colours the message? Did she not want to add an adult perspective? Some words of reassurance? Ask me how I felt?

Nope, just, 'the cat was out of the bag'.

In other words, my sister had done the dirty work for her. Okay, so maybe it wasn't the ideal method of revelation, but it saved her the trouble. One more thankless task out of the way. Could she not have sat us both down, or all three of us? A family meeting around the fire? Anything other than the cat was out of the god-damned bag?

I did ask my mother all sorts of questions about myself so I suppose it's plausible that she thought I would eventually ask about being adopted. But when the years slipped by – over a decade – and I didn't say one word, did that not seem odd? I find it unlikely that she would have forgotten, more likely, she missed her moment. Words left unsaid get harder to say. They grow in the mouth, too big to let loose.

She had no idea that my universe ripped apart that day, my own Big Bang. How could she? She didn't ask. It was cowardly of her not to ask.

Leah's bombshell and the cat's exit from the bag coincided with my awareness of my mother's undiagnosed depression, which was marked by her spending the majority of her time in bed where she sat, like a ball of melon in a melon baller, the mattress spooning around her. She emerged from the bedroom solely to cook and perform rudimentary housework.

But like a functioning alcoholic, she slavishly adhered to routines. The loveless meals that she robotically produced were her reason and lifeline. She could prove to herself that she was coping because she managed these basic requirements of family life each day. If she cleared those hurdles, she was doing her job, she was fine.

Leah's disclosure conveniently represented one less problem to solve, one less seemingly insurmountable task ticked off an endless list. Or maybe she really didn't think it was that big a deal, or at least convinced herself that was so. In order to move forward in those days, to force one heavy foot in front of the other, she needed blinkers lashed firmly in place.

This latest data drop from my brother, that my mother had actively hidden information from me, reinforced my runt of the litter feeling. The resources were depleted, the novelty well-worn off, by the time it came to me. I felt overshadowed and overlooked again.

But at least, I thought, the cat was out of the bag for good; there were to be no more surprises.

4

I'M NO MOZART (1993–98)

Until I was a teenager, I didn't have any conscious adoption fantasies. If I thought about my 'first' family, it was in purely biological, hereditary terms: where did the drop of water on the end of my nose come from? It's a small button of cartilage that sticks out from the bottom of my nose that can resemble a droplet of water in certain light. My siblings, convinced it was a pimple, tried to pop it for me when we were kids. I thought of poking cartilage or my curly hair as discrete genes or physical characteristics separate from the rest of me, in the same way we tend to separate body from mind.

My creation story, my aetiology and genesis began like anyone else's, when girl met boy. In my case, when Ruth Bolan met Seymour 'Sy' Freed. The possibility of me, as I am today, came about only because these two particular people met at a specific time and place, my parents own 'meet-cute'. And, despite all that I know now, that is still largely true.

And so, my story started in 1956 when a niece of my maternal grandmother's, Bunny, and her husband Jerry, who was a cousin of my father's, ran into my grandparents at a local restaurant in Boston. When Nana and Papa commented that Ruth was living in Brooklyn, Jerry mentioned my father, also a denizen of Brooklyn, and they were given Ruth's number to pass onto Sy. The only person who was left out of all this mentioning and calling of Ruth, was Ruth herself. Her mother, and it would have been Nana, neglected to mention it to her. 'Call this girl,' Bunny and Jerry instructed Sy in the way of pushy relatives throughout time.

Ruth was living with two other single, professional women in the only Art Deco apartment building on Henry Street in Brooklyn Heights. They had recently been bombarded with heavy breathing, obscene phone calls. When my father, a softly spoken, civil engineer dutifully called, he did not receive, in the words of my mother, a cordial response:

'Who is this? Why are you calling? I'm going to call the police if you don't stop ringing this number!' she threatened.

It took some confusing minutes for the Bunny connection to penetrate but it eventually hit its mark and either out of embarrassment or relief, my mother agreed to a date.

'He was the only person I knew in New York City who owned a car,' my mother enthused years later, a quality she would depend upon and value for the rest of her life.

For their first date, Sy drove her out to Long Island, to a place called Swan Lake for dinner and dancing. Ruth wrote about the date:

I, and I think Sy had a very nice time. I was, however, leaving for a three-week vacation in Boston and wondered if for both of us we would not remember each other. But we did. Sy called as soon as I came back to NY and we began dating regularly ... I think Sy liked having a girlfriend who lived relatively near where he did. No more long trips to the Bronx and other places. For me, Sy surpassed in quality anyone I had previously dated long enough

to know reasonably well. He was extremely thoughtful, very easy
to talk to and get along with and lacking the egocentricity that I
had previously encountered.

That night at Swan Lake was the last time they went dancing but they were engaged and married six months later.

When I asked her about the proposal, my mother told me
that she didn't recall a specific time or place. With typically
understated pragmatism she said, 'I think we agreed that it
seemed like the next logical step.'

There was, however, a ring, Hannah's – Sy's recently
deceased mother – old world diamond reset in updated
platinum, and an engagement party. In the photos, Ruth is
bright-eyed and smiling, but also camera-shy and awkward,
her arms pinned back over the formal, tailored dress.

I know little about my father's prior dating habits except
what can be gleaned from 'the Bronx and other places' reference and his photo albums. A slim, bathing-suited blonde is
posed next to a pole on the beach at Coney Island, 'Which
one is the pole?' reads the caption in precise, capital letters.

My mother had been briefly engaged to an Israeli man,
Chaim. She first tells me this as we sit on the Brooklyn
Heights promenade after walking past the still bright red
door of her old building, around the corner from where I
was then living.

'He had very sexy eyes,' she says of the fiancé. 'I don't
know what he saw in me; he thought I was soft and naive.' I
sputter at the thought of my fearsome mother as a wide-eyed
innocent but I suppose this was a more carefree time in her
life. Pictures prove her to have been a very pretty, Elizabeth
Taylor type with a becoming pixie-ish haircut and guileless
blue eyes.

Chaim had grown up in the stark landscape of a nascent

Israel and considered my mother's friends and pursuits as frivolous and trivial.

Later she would send me an email with the subject line: The Penultimate Boyfriend to be followed by Courtship and Marriage:

> At the beginning of junior year of college I went to a Hillel mixer and met Chaim who was in his first year at Harvard Business School . . . Born in Vienna, he left with his older brother shortly after the annexation of Austria. The last time he saw his parents was when they put Chaim and his brother with a group of children on a train, the first leg of an illegal journey to Israel . . . they evaded the British and landed in Israel. He was separated from his brother, raised in a children's village, learned carpentry, served in the army and started college. Somehow Hadassah [the Women's Zionist Organization of America founded in 1912 to promote Jewish values] took an interest in him and arranged for him to complete his undergraduate education at Columbia University . . . I don't think we really understood each other particularly well but in spite of a break up or two the relationship persisted . . . whatever problems I was struggling with seemed so minuscule compared to both the past and present issues in his life that I never felt a great amount of closeness or trust in him.

Well, thank goodness for that otherwise I might not have been me! Thank you, Bunny and Jerry Barclay for pushing! Thank you, Sy, for calling and persisting through the hectoring and the threats! Thank you, obscene phone callers for the part you played! Thank you Ruth for saying yes! Thank you to that car, the chariot to my future!

In high school, I would meet my best friend Nora on Saturdays. We trawled the record shops and second-hand and goodwill shops looking for pointy-toed vintage heels and tweed overcoats; we perused the makeup section of Woolworth's but mostly we sat and talked over coffee and cigarettes in the food court at the mall. Nora funded the coffee and cigarettes despite me working every school holiday and vacation at my father's office, Nab Construction in Queens. At the end of each work week, I was obliged to turn over my pay to my mother for safe-keeping. A tradition that was steeped in her innate thrift and the 'little me too' scenario.

For my 9th birthday – which was celebrated! – I received a short-lived allowance. I was given five cents every Sunday. I saved my coins in a clear plastic box, sometimes exchanging five nickels for a quarter, but I enjoyed the heft of the coins and never exchanged them for dollar bills. The coins were a collection with a value of their own, they represented trust and autonomy.

By summer, I had amassed a modest sum. My sister and I would hop on a bus in the morning and get off at the Saxon Woods pool where we spent the days splashing around and lying on the concrete surrounded by the smell of chlorine, urine and fried food. We brought a bag lunch and were not given money for fripperies like burgers and fries.

One hot day, it finally dawned on me, at my sister's suggestion, what I had been saving up for: ice cream! After shaking the water out of our ears, groggy from too many underwater somersaults and too much sun, it was heavenly to sit on the now abandoned loungers, licking sweet vanilla from a dripping cone or burping out the nose-fizzing, sarsaparilla gas from a root beer. This was my first taste of consumer freedom, the spending power of my very own cash. I had saved each and every penny all through the spring and now here was something I wanted and I could treat my big sister to.

All perfectly reasonable, you might think. But no, my

mother did not think so. It could not possibly have been my idea or my choice, I must have done it because Leah said to. I had been coerced like a vulnerable pensioner swindled out of their savings by ruthless criminals. My allowance was abruptly ended.

Before handing over my Nab Construction pay packet one day, I had the temerity to ask if I might keep two of my dollars.

'What for?'

'Deodorant.'

'Take a bath,' she said and dropped the envelope in her bedside table drawer.

It was during those marathon discussions with Nora that I first started talking about being adopted and fantasised about meeting my birth mother. It was actually more of an anti-fantasy. I imagined a woman living in a ranch-style house somewhere out on Long Island, the suburbs that stretch east of Brooklyn and Queens. All the brown plaid furniture would be fitted with custom plastic slip-covers. There would be beige, wall-to-wall shag carpeting. The woman who answered my knock at the door would be wearing a turtleneck and flared trousers or a muumuu. She would have wiry grey hair, garish blue eyeshadow and an ashtray on a chain around her neck. 'Sure,' she would say, with palpable disinterest, 'I gave a kid up for adoption. Was that you?' the haze from the twin streams of cigarette smoke flowing from her nose merging with the frizz of her hair.

And I would say, 'thank you for not aborting me! You made a great decision; I have a wonderful life!'

I didn't have anyone particular in mind in the role of my father but I was equally keen to thank him too. Surely they'd want to know that I was happy, I reasoned. Nora, always the wiser of the two of us, pointed out that my birth might have been a traumatic time in this man or woman's life. Fair enough, I thought. So, despite my undeniable and understandable curiosity, and since I was so purportedly happy, I could carry on without this grand gesture.

In my twenties my conversations with my mother became as wide-ranging as they had been with Nora. While preparing Thanksgiving dinner one year, I asked if it had been a difficult decision to adopt.

'It would have been simpler to do it ourselves,' my mother said. 'There were things we could have done,' she added but she didn't think any invasive medical procedures were warranted. In the 1960s, it would have been presumed that any conception problems lay with her alone; a man's ability to father children was rarely, if ever, questioned.

In Dani Shapiro's memoir *Inheritance* about finding out that her father was not her biological father and she was instead the daughter of a sperm donor, she discovered that her parents went to the Farris Institute for Parenthood in Pennsylvania for what was called 'confused artificial insemination,' a practice that consisted of mixing the father's sperm with sperm from a donor.

If my mother had been willing to undergo more invasive procedures, perhaps she too might have been led to the Farris Institute for Parenthood, but Ruth claimed that neither she nor my father felt the need to pass down their own genes. 'Our genes weren't so special, we're not geniuses; I'm no Mozart!' she protested.

She also didn't have any interest in clones. She opined that a lot of people want to see themselves in their children, but she had no need of that.

'There are different ways to make a family,' was how my father put it.

Adoption made sense to both of them and so did Louise

Wise Services, the pre-eminent Jewish adoption agency in New York City. Wise by name and wise by nature, or so was the public image. Their guiding principle, in line with the zeitgeist, was that nurture was far more important than nature in the development of a child.

They took this stated principle to an extreme and were sued because of it. Nurture was so influential that they failed to disclose any history of mental illness or institutionalisations, omissions they vigorously and repeatedly denied when these questionable practices came to light. This stance had the added benefit to the agency that any negative outcomes as far as the adoptions were concerned lay with the quality of nurture provided by the adoptive parents.

However, privately, or more accurately, secretly, Louise Wise Services was involved in a long-term study of twins and triplets which they separated at birth in an attempt to answer the perennial 'nature verses nurture' question. The study itself, which commenced in 1961 – my brother's year of birth – was devised by one Dr Peter Neubauer, a lauded child psychiatrist and psychoanalyst who was at that time director of New York's Child Development Center. Neubauer had escaped to Switzerland from Nazi-occupied Austria, where he completed his psychiatric training at the University of Bern in 1941, emigrating to America, land of opportunity, later that year where he joined the staff at New York's Bellevue Hospital. This date and point of embarkation of his emigration will turn out to be the first in a host of coincidences in my life.

Tim Wardle's documentary, *Three Identical Strangers* tells the extraordinary story of a set of triplets who were separated at birth and placed for adoption with three different families in New York State. Louise Wise Services told the adoptive parents that their baby boys were part of an on-going study and researchers would be visiting and observing their children at regular intervals. If they wanted the boys, these were the conditions. They were not told that the boys were triplets. They were not told that they were subjects of a long-term, secret study that continued into the 1980s.

I attended the London premiere of the film with Orna, a friend of mine from high school who had worked at Triplets Roumanian Steakhouse, the Lower East Side restaurant that the reunited triplets had opened in 1988. Above and beyond the horror of the film's revelations, I was overcome with gratitude that my parents had passed away by then and had no knowledge of this vast scandal.

After the triplets were reunited in 1980, the three sets of parents held a meeting with Louise Wise Services to get some answers. It was standard practice, they were told, to separate twins and triplets. This was true; starting in the 1950s Dr Viola Bernard, Louise Wise Services' Chief Psychiatrist, high-handedly decided that multiple children would be too much of a burden for the adoptive mothers to cope with. These lesser parents, who already couldn't produce their own children, evidently couldn't be trusted to look after more than one child at a time. There was absolutely no mention of the study.

The meeting took place on a rainy evening and the father of Bobby, one of the triplets, returned to Louise Wise Services to retrieve an umbrella he had left behind. When he slipped back in, he witnessed the staff cracking open a bottle of champagne, toasting their good escape; the parents had left none the wiser about the study. I would bet big money that Barbara Miller, whom my brother met around the same time, was one of those raising a glass in that room.

'How do you think my father felt when he saw that?' Bobby asked me.

Tim Wardle told me that although some have argued that psychology was still in its unregulated infancy and it was like the wild west, Peter Neubauer and his Child Development Center had approached other adoption agencies who had turned him down due to the very questionable morality of the proposed study. While it is true that the idea of informed consent had not yet entered research circles, how difficult would it have been to decide that a study that entails playing God with children, separating them at birth, and placing them in different socio-economic circumstances so you can chart their development isn't ethical? Again, if it wasn't shameful, why was it kept secret?

But it was also a secret in plain sight. There was a team of researchers who would routinely observe the children at regular intervals, having them perform tasks and play games and cataloguing the results. And then there was Peter Neubauer himself who, according to a friend of mine who knew him socially in the 1980s and '90s, regaled brunch guests with stories of how one twin put ketchup all over all of his food and then the other twin miles and worlds away would do just the same. Neubauer even mentioned the study in a trade book he published, as did his colleague, Dr Samuel Abrams.

None of this was public knowledge when my parents were adopting, and in order to create their family, my parents went in hope and trust to Louise Wise to be granted young lives to nurture into a family of their own.

As cultural, rather than religious Jews, a Jewish adoption agency was the right fit. Nana always accused Ruth of being a snob. From Nana's point of view, it was all well and good to be book smart but could you cook a decent meal and no, Ruth most certainly could not. Nana wasn't so far off the mark as Ruth was a bit of an intellectual snob. In adopting a baby whose birth mother was Jewish, my mother could assume that the woman was most likely educated and similar to herself in life outlook and aims. So while she didn't need a clone of herself, she was looking for children from a similar clan, a 'member of the tribe' as the saying goes.

When I asked if she had been told anything about my birth parents, she said, 'I think they were students at Queens College.'

This was a story that suited all parties. Whether it was tailored by Louise Wise Services to appeal to my parents, or if Ruth made it up to assuage me, who can say. It was brilliantly innocuous. It conjured an image of two co-eds, bright young aspirational things, not yet ready to settle down. Ruth briefly actually taught Psychology – not Child Psychology – at Queens College, so it was an image we could all believe in. As it so happens, *nothing* could have been further from the truth.

It came to light in another of these conversations with my mother that I was, in fact, a surprise. Obviously not in the traditional sense of an unplanned pregnancy, at least to this set of parents. Abortion was still illegal in 1967 but even so, there were still more childless parents than parent-less children. Yet, despite being actively discouraged by Louise Wise Services, my parents ploughed on and 'put in for a third child' in my mother's words. I have no idea why they thought three was the magic number.

My brother has knowledge of the record of the social worker's first visit to my parents' one bedroom apartment in Queens. There was classical music playing on the stereo and the apartment was messy. Having warned my parents that the odds were not in their favour when they applied for a second child, a social worker was dutifully dispatched to vet the new home – they had bought a small house by this time – and check on the welfare of their first charge.

Other than the location, little else had changed. The lackadaisical approach to housekeeping persisted as did the classical music in the background, but there was one clearly very welcome addition: a thriving, precocious, blue-eyed boy and so ... they were granted Leah.

Only at my parents' insistence did Louise Wise capitulate and agree to process their application for a third child as a courtesy. The same social worker – who my mother described as 'older, perhaps in her fifties, European, formal, not overly bright and susceptible, I thought, to subtle flattery' – was dispatched to the unkempt Queens house, her mind firmly set against a further placement. It would not only be against the agency's advice but there were deserving couples begging for babies with pristine homes in the leafy suburbs. She had not, however, reckoned on my future siblings.

Paul, at six, was even more voluble and endearing than he'd been at three, his lashes grown longer and more effectively batted. A recent addition to his charm offensive was the violin. His career in music, which continues to this day, had just begun by way of the Suzuki Method and he leapt at the opportunity to play 'Twinkle, Twinkle Little Star' for the 'nice lady' on his violin. My three-year-old sister-to-be sat quietly flicking through the *New York Times* throughout my brother's performance and afterwards commented to the social worker that she had an unusual license plate.

My fate was sealed and I became the exception to the Louise Wise rule. Twins and triplets were separated but the Freeds got three children. Perhaps it is more accurate to say that I was an exception as opposed to a surprise, and as my brother before me heard 'chosen,' I chose to hear 'exceptional', but I owed that same status to my siblings.

Throughout my twenties, every once in a while the urge to look for my birth parents would crop up. Sometimes I would go so far as to ask Paul to remind me of the name of the lady at the adoption agency but as soon as Barbara Miller's name was invoked, so were her damning words. They were a perfect deterrent as there was always some real or perceived drama in my life: I needed to find a place to live, or a job, I was dating some guy, I wasn't dating some guy, my apartment was broken into, I broke a finger, I broke a nail. Searching for birth parents is a bit like having a baby, there's never a perfect time.

Similar to my mother's stance on people desiring to see themselves reflected in their children, I felt that people who were looking for their biological parents were really looking for themselves. In finding their family, they hoped to find some clue to themselves. I didn't think there were clues to me that I would find beyond myself, embodied in other people. I have to admit that I looked upon these seekers and their need with some disdain. And wanting to find someone who looked like me felt somewhat frivolous, it didn't seem like a good enough reason to upend their lives and mine.

I can also say that there are certain enjoyments and freedoms to be had in knowing nothing about your birth family. Mom and Uncle Lew were both short and slightly stocky with sturdy, muscular legs. As he got older, Lew became a bit forgetful and repetitive. A favourite refrain was, 'You know early Alzheimer's runs in our family!' I was equally repetitive in my catty response: 'Early Alzheimer's might run in *your* short, squat family, not mine!

And it was easy for me to forget that we weren't related. I felt extremely connected to my family, fiercely and almost wilfully so. My friend Kate is the oldest of four kids and she looks a lot like her mother. Each of her siblings is a different iteration of the same look, variations on a theme, like Russian nesting dolls.

'At least you can look at your mother and know that you're going to age well. I don't think I will,' I told her.

'Why, because your mother hasn't? Do you think her DNA seeped into you through osmosis or proximity? Besides, she's never even used moisturiser!' Harsh, perhaps, but fair!

But, as I pointed out to Kate, I had never seen anyone who looked like me. 'Except for Judy Davis, and if Judy Davis was my birth mother, I'd drop Ruth like a hot potato!' I said.

Once it popped out of my mouth, it struck me as true enough. It's not that I'm particularly unusual looking and neither am I face-blind, on the contrary I consider myself reasonably observant. I suppose it is possible that the disruption to the bonding and attachment process with my birth mother might have warped my facial recognition ability. Nevertheless, I had never met anyone who looked like me and the Australian actress Judy Davis with her curly hair and small, bright blue eyes was the closest I'd come.

Finally, I had a fully-fledged adoption fantasy! I wholeheartedly embraced the idea of Judy Davis as my birth mother, happily disregarding the fact that she would have been twelve at the time of my birth and if I was anything to go by, early puberty did not run in our family. It is exceedingly difficult to imagine under what circumstances I would have ended up in a Jewish adoption agency in New York when Judy grew up a strict Catholic in Perth. However, these were mere trifling details, the larger picture was the stuff of a diverting fantasy that Judy Davis herself had indulged in. In *High Tide* (1987) Judy Davis plays a woman who is drawn to a teenage girl she encounters by chance before she realises that the girl is her daughter who she abandoned as an infant! Judy Davis, are you my mirror?

And so, in my late twenties I embarked, with the help of my amused parents, on writing a play, *Judy Davis Is My*

Mother, An Adoption Fantasy. The one-act, one-woman play takes place in the green room of *The Oprah Winfrey Show.* A sixteen-year-old-girl paces the room, anxiously waiting to be reunited, live on television, with her mother, Judy Davis.

Judy Davis as a birth mother fantasy was safe for all of us. *My Brilliant Career* was a favourite film of my mother's and one of the first I ever saw in the cinema with my parents. The character in my play could be Judy's character in the film, the feisty and rebellious Sybylla Melvyn with her strong, creative desires. Even so, the girl who walked round and round that green room in my play was nervous. 'Will Judy like me?' she worried.

My parents helped me remember my teenage years as seen from the outside. They revelled in recounting the terrors I put them through, able to laugh with the distance of years. This was another foray into seeing ourselves through each other's eyes and another way to bring us closer.

What were you like as kids? I asked my parents. What was your home life like? My father, when asked his age, still maintained that he was seventeen. At seventeen, he was halfway through college, having graduated high school two and a half years early. Shortly after that, he was sent to the Philippines with the Army Corps of Engineers as part of the Korean War effort. Of his childhood, he said that his father was the only Jew in their Williamsburg, Brooklyn neighbourhood to keep homing pigeons, all the other guys who kept homing pigeons were Italian, and that Bubbles Silverman, who grew up to be opera singer Beverly Sills, lived in the same building.

My mother was more forthcoming and for my thirtieth birthday, wrote me a series of essays 'since you asked,' she said.

'Fragments of an Early Life' was the first missive, which comprised seven hand-written pages. It starts in 1937 when she is five years old. There is only one entry for 1938:

I am in first grade. For the first time I select a book from the class library. Although I have never seen this book before, I can read all the words. I am very excited. It is perhaps the highlight of the year.

One entry from 1939 reads:

The class bully has persistently been pulling my hair, stepping on my toes and pushing me down on the way home from school. I don't tell anyone but I can't eat breakfast and dread going to school. Somehow the school finds out. The solution is that he is kept in ten minutes to give me a head start on my trip home.

Another entry for that year reads:

I am told (years later) that for some time I have been making a nuisance of myself seeing wild animals in my room at night. I remember only one incident. I wake up in a dark and silent room. They are there, menacing and ready to pounce. I put on my slippers and go to my parents' room intending to wake them. But I don't. I sit on the rug at the side of their bed until first light. When I go back to my room the animals have departed, never to return.

She emerges as a rather shy, bookish girl, sometimes shamed and taunted. Her feelings of being a disappointment are reflected in her own disillusionment with the adults in her life. It was not a warm household.

What isn't expressed but seeps through her writing is the anti-Semitism that was the main cause of the bullying, that while she was born Ruth Bolanski, her brother, seven years later, was born Lewis Bolan. The family named shortened to sound less Jewish when they moved to Worcester and her father became the manager of a supermarket with no other Jewish employees. She also fails to mention that he mismanaged the market into the ground. Her focus is on her up and out: Wellesley College.

She concludes the handwritten section with, 'To be continued maybe' in pencil.

Included in the same envelope are ten typed pages entitled 'Wellesley College 1950–1954' and written as an essay, which concludes:

And so, ready or not, I left Wellesley. I would begin an independent life, responsible for myself. All my decisions for better or worse would be mine to make and live with.

5

NEWS AT 10 (2002)

Most children can look at their inception and see a love story. Clearly it isn't always the case, but from a kid's point of view, your parents generally got together for the express purpose of having you. For adopted children, things are not quite so straightforward, though I do view Ruth and Sy as crucial to my formation if not my creation.

If, as Buddhists believe, we choose our parents, adopted people go about it in a circuitous fashion. And because of that indirect route which brought you to your parents, because you are not the direct fruit of their love, because of the fork in your young road, because of that detour, because you were passed by unseen hands along a human chain to get to your parents, because of this cast of unseen actors shadowing the figures in your life, there is an over-riding feeling for adopted children that our stories are not our own. How can you own your story when you don't know your story? You are like a tree in a child's drawing, coming straight out of the ground with no roots. You cannot trace that straight line from meeting to marriage to baby carriage.

You are at the intersection of opposing stories, one story of a meeting and conception and another story of meeting and no conception. You fill the interstice between these stories, a crevice that is filled with disappointment and desire. At some critical point you were judged to be undesirable, or at the very least inconvenient, by the person or persons who had the power to decide for you. You were a problem to be solved, or more optimistically, a gift to be bestowed. The unknown detours that you took turned upon the dramatic spikes in the lives of others. The biggest reasons of why and who you are, are the high points and low points of other actors in your young life. You are not the lead. Your story is their story; your story is written in their scars.

In a sealed adoption, you do not know the larger narratives that produced you; a love story, an affair, a rape, a broken condom, a drunken office party. And then the unexpected-ness of you and the unwantedness of you. The conveyance of you and then your availability to attach to someone else's story. A story of we tried for years, of failed IVF, of we left it too late, of we wanted to adopt, a tale of 'we saw a need'. You are the axis upon which other people's stories turn.

If there were words of hope and longing spoken about you before you were born, they were interrupted. There was a moment when those words changed. And then there were appointments with doctors, nurses, social workers, adoption agents, fosterers and judges and a cascade of paperwork to change the tide of your fortunes. You rode in at the turning of the tides, waves of despair washing in as waves of hope and expectation wash out.

'I found my mother! News at 10!' I was at work when I saw Paul's email to me and Leah.

On the eve of his wedding in 1989, Paul decided to aban-don his search for his birth mother. In hindsight, we can be relatively confident that Barbara Miller never honoured his request to log his interest in reunion on New York State's Adoption and Medical Information Registry. Even so, he was starting a new chapter in his life and had reached the conclusion that he no longer needed or wanted to find this woman whom he had never met. He would walk forward in his life, with baggage of course, but he would enter his marriage with his own achievements, hopes and dreams.

But time chips away at our staunchest resolves and here was an email in 2002: I found my mother! There was an immediate volley of excited and confused emails until Paul wrote, 'I didn't speak to her, Rachel did. It's not really my story, I should let her tell it.'

Picture me as Wile E. Coyote desperately galloping after the details of this tale, grasping arms outstretched until I read the words 'it's not really my story.' As abruptly as Wile E. Coyote when he finally sees the cliff in front of him, I lean back, heels foremost, clouds of dust rising as I apply the brakes.

How is this not Paul's story? Surely, if ever there was a story that was yours – being reunited with your birth mother – that story should be your story. At least it should be half your story. You should figure somewhere in the narrative, some part of this tale should be yours. Your name should at least feature in the credits. You should not be a silent partner, a footnote or an 'also ran' in this story!

'It's not my story, it's Rachel's story,' both exasperated me and temporarily extinguished any interest in his story that was not his. How is finding your birth mother someone else's story?

There are many strands to the web that connects me and my siblings but the adopted lark is a big shared experience. If it wasn't his story, it couldn't be ours. He had not spoken to his mother, and yet his wife had spoken to her twice.

The story, such as it was, had now been reduced to hearsay, admittedly very interesting hearsay, but hearsay nevertheless. As it happened, one of their children had been given a possible diagnosis of Crohn's Disease and they were wondering if it might be hereditary. My brother had bypassed the formidable mistress of obfuscation, Barbara Miller, and hired a private detective who swiftly identified his birth mother, inclusive of telephone number.

The detective advised Paul that it would be better for his wife to make the initial contact with the woman to confirm that she was indeed his mother. The circumstances of the pregnancy were unknown and my brother's voice might resemble his birth father's, which might in turn trigger bad memories and risk endangering the possibility of a reunion before it started. Of course, the detective was right to be cautious but again, Paul, the adopted party, was the problem. His voice was the liability, the problem to be solved.

So, Rachel called Paul's mother and followed the carefully worded script provided by the gumshoe: 'My husband was born on June 24, 1961, does that date mean anything to you?' I stowed these tactful words of introduction away for later use.

The woman who answered the phone left a long pause before answering, 'No,' that date did not mean anything to her and then she hung up.

'That's normal,' consoled the detective. 'Call again and tell her there is a health concern and that it's important to find out if it features in the family tree.'

In that case, Paul's mother admitted, when Rachel called back, that date did mean something to her and that in fact, she gave birth to a boy on that day but no, there was no history of Crohn's that she was aware of which ran in the family.

It occurred to me many years later, as I stood on the brink

of making my own phone calls, that my brother might well have been reluctant to put himself forward to this woman for reasons beyond the concerns stated by the detective. The threat of rejection is the sword of Damocles that looms over adoption reunions. That first, flat denial was the dreaded slice.

Being reunited with your birth family is rarely accidental. This is not 'bumping into someone' or a 'fancy meeting you here' type of coincidence. Even if the reunion is welcome it is not a random happenstance. This is exposure of a seminal link to the one person from your past you are unlikely to forget.

It is easy to imagine a woman reflexively turning away from that first, unbidden contact but it is still a hurtful echo of that initial rejection. I imagine I would also be quick to resentment. Who are you to reject me? A bitterness rooted in the fact that, as ever, they have the power in this situation, to accept or deny you.

Reunion with birth family is a moment of fraught tension, the type of tension that precedes peace talks. On the surface it looks like adults meeting each other as supposed equals but underneath, the primal mind is in charge, that ancient part of us filled with longing and desire but primed for fight or flight at the slightest blink. So, for Paul and his mother, to have begun with an indirect approach, dishonesty and deception – or anything that could be so interpreted – didn't merely risk 'getting off on the wrong foot'.

Needless to say, my sister, mother and I picked over the bones of my brother's story. My mother felt, and I agreed, that it must have been awful for Paul's mother to be called out of the blue and manipulated into admitting maternity by a daughter-in-law she never even knew she had. I don't know if Ruth also felt that, because Paul was looking for his birth mother, this woman would think Ruth had failed him. While I did have sympathy for his birth mother, I also felt that the way in which the reunion was conducted denied both her and Paul the emotional ownership over the reunion. The pretext for the reunion pre-empted the reunion.

There was also still a competitive advantage within our family in agreeing with Ruth. I'm not sure where our competitive relationships developed. My mother derided rather than encouraged the expression of our competitiveness as siblings, but she did desire for her children to do well and to succeed — as opposed to be happy or fulfilled, for example — and success is necessarily a comparative and therefore competitive business. And while she didn't look outwardly like she cared a fig for what people thought of her, that only went so far.

From Dani Shapiro's book, I got the sense that early sperm donors, like her birth father, didn't think that they had really fathered a child because they didn't physically have sex with the mother, hadn't even so much as bought her a drink. But what other purpose could there have been to donating the sperm, what other outcome? And in her case, the donor was a medical student. Then again, pregnancy does have that dramatic element of surprise. I'm sure there were countless adoption cases where the fathers were genuinely unaware that their trysts, affairs and romances also resulted in pregnancy. They too did not think they had fathered a child.

But mothers have to know. It's the reason that Judaism, the 'show me' religion, passes through the mother. Because we know and she knows, regardless of who the father may be, she is unquestionably the mother because the baby came out of her womb.

Letters and information were slowly exchanged between Paul and his mother as he stepped into the lead role in his story. She was mystified about his musical talent, definitely not from her, she said. She had had a relationship with a tall, blond, divorced man who did not want to get re-married when she became pregnant. After giving up Paul, she went on to marry and give birth to other children. She had kept Paul's birth secret from her husband, now deceased, and children. She had done what she thought would be best for Paul and viewed getting married and having legitimate children as a second, respectable chance, a do-over.

The most common reason for adoptees to search for their birth family – and one I have always shared – is to find people who bear a physical similarity to you. If you have always been surrounded by family resemblance, it is part of the fabric of your life, you don't notice it. Fundamental to belonging, this likeness is a product of genes but also environment, these looks are shaped by where your family lives and what your family eats and thereby represents everything that adopted people perceive that we're missing, that sense of belonging just because you are there. Everyone in your purview is a mirror of you, you are reflected in their faces.

It was a shock to see a picture of Paul's mother – my brother's teeth grinning from her mouth, his eyes twinkling in her face, a feminine distortion of my brother.

Almost a decade after the first phone call, there was a meeting. Paul's mother arrived in 'slimming' black. 'You look just like my son,' she told him without a hint of irony.

Do you dare to dream for a child you said goodbye to? Do you regret? Does your love close over like a fist shoved deep inside a pocket? Do you say 'it was for the best' like a mantra until you forget in the rush of the rest of your life? So long ago and so many times since, she must have told herself that this baby, now this man, was not her son, that she could lay no claim to him now.

In the photographs of their reunion, their smiling apple cheeks and their toothy, face-splitting, Cheshire grins are identical. Rachel and their youngest son complete the picture. They look like a family, three generations of connected paper dolls, a common set of features splashed across them.

To look like someone, to resemble seemed forbidden and delicious. Despite taking a dim view of my brother's need to find and meet his birth mother, I was jealous of his physical similarity to her. I wanted familial resemblance in something other than verbal tics and physical habits, shared stories, a common sense of both humour and outrage and a nose for conspiracy. I wanted actual traits, a tendency to pronate, long fingers and toes, small patellas, the curly hair and the drip of cartilage. I wanted to see how I fitted together, which of my constituent parts came from others, what mingled together to make me.

Oddly enough, Ruth longed for this too. 'Why do all my grandchildren look like the other parent and not my child?' she moaned. As if they were somehow less her grandchildren if they didn't look like her son or daughter. She who adopted three strangers and called them her children. She didn't live long enough to see Dexter as a teenager and although it is true that he looks more like my husband, Simon, he does look a bit like me. It also turns out that he bears a striking resemblance to the man who I have discovered is my own birth father.

More of his family tree has been revealed to my brother through 23andMe searches, as it has for so many. Fathers un-become fathers and long-hidden relationships and slips are exposed when the big DNA rock is lifted.

From our oldest civilizations, we have kept track of our ancestors, tracing our histories and the stories of ourselves through our connections to each other, the family trees through which our lineage and lands, our languages and loyalties all pass, these degrees of connection and slim separations. There may only be six degrees of separation, but it is the connections that always count first; it is our connections to our tribes and our people that we always fall back on. We are, in part, defined by our family fortunes and it is in future generations of family that we invest.

The Church of Latter-day Saints has collected ancestral information since 1894, long before DNA tests and mutual consent registries, in order to connect with dead relatives and invite them to join the church on a voluntary, posthumous basis so that they may all be sealed together in heaven. Their work was a forerunner to companies such as Ancestry.com and a host of others. The internet and social media have supercharged the leg work that used to entail sleuthing at the library and laboriously poring through phone books and death registers.

As a result of all this unearthed history, sealed adoptions were prized open by private detectives, especially in cases where consent paperwork failed to get filed for one reason or another. Like bounty hunters, once a subject is identified, it is their job to find the current whereabouts of the birth parents or child, preferably alive or sadly dead.

The purpose of these sealed adoptions was to protect the privacy of the birth mothers and their families, but who owns a secret? Who has the rights to it? Whatever Louise Wise Services chose to say about my birth was set in stone in 1967 and cannot be unsaid, disproved or exposed. I still have to abide by their rules.

When Paul found his mother, I was thirty-five and newly married. I didn't feel the siren call to find my birth family. The payoff of finding his mother didn't seem worth the risk of offending Ruth: not that she professed any offence, but I was habitually conditioned to avoid causing any.

I was also still trying to pin down my evolving story, so when my friend Douglas suggested a Gotham Writers

Workshop in memoir writing, I returned to writing to explore my formative history. I wanted to make sense of it, make it mine, have it come from me, be told by me. I wanted to own my story.

I sent my parents a copy of the sixteen-page piece about how I found out that I was adopted. In return, I received a letter from my mother with spelling corrections and 'some minor factual corrections'. One of which was that my father had a Master of Civil Engineering and not a Ph.D and she 'wasn't really a child psychologist'. Another important correction she felt I needed to know was that 'Your father didn't cook. For a while, however, he broiled steaks in the fireplace on Sundays. Otherwise cooking = take out (that he was good at).'

She concluded that it was 'an emotionally honest, sensitive, well-written meditation on the mixture of adoption-driven family life crossed with issues that presumably could occur without benefit of atypical beginnings.' This was the entire scope of her comments; she did not comment on my depiction of her parenting skills or my theory that I hadn't been told I was adopted because she couldn't be bothered.

I was desperately relieved that she didn't hate it or me. It felt like a small but important, rather momentous, step outside of the shadow of her image and her image of me. I had the confidence that her love was robust, and so I had the courage and the need to say that I had been hurt and disappointed by finding out instead of being told by her, and that this loomed large in me. That she approved this step into my own light, validated the faith I had blindly put in her.

PART II

The sandwood...

PART II

The sandwiched mother

6

START SPREADING
THE NEWS (2004)

'I'm pregnant, I'm pregnant,' thrummed through me all day at work like an extra heartbeat, one that I knew beat within me but I couldn't yet feel. It is still pulsing through me when we meet Douglas at The Urge. 'Can I get a vodka tonic and a seltzer with lime?' I holler over the deafening unz, unz, unz of the music to the bare-chested bartender.

'Seltzer? Are you pregnant?' Douglas asks.

I've made it to the three-month mark, but at thirty-six, I am an 'older mother' and at higher risk of having a baby with chromosomal disorders so we were waiting for the results of the amniocentesis before telling anyone. Too surprised to disguise my delight, my attempt at an inscru-table Mona Lisa smile dissolved into a huge grin. This cat's out of the bag!

At the time, 2004, it was just as unreasonably difficult to find a gynaecologist accepting new patients in New York as it was to get a face-to-face doctor's appointment in Covid-blighted Britain. Demand for OB/GYN services remained constant but supply was inexplicably threadbare.

After months of fruitless phoning around, I eventually hit the trifecta, finding one that not only accepted my insurance but new patients as well and whose office was within walking distance of mine. As an added bonus, she was a woman. I once had a male gynaecologist whose hands were the size of meat-cleavers and just as delicate. She was all business and conducted my initial appointment as if it were a job interview.

'Where do you see your ovaries in five years?'

'You're married, what are you waiting for, you're thirty-six!'

'Have you been trying?'

'For how long?'

She hammered me with rapid-fire questions.

'Not seriously, not for long,' I told her defensively, 'maybe five months.'

'Five months! I want some tests,' she said. 'First you, then your husband.'

And while that was technically true, until the last of those months, my commitment to the 'trying' had been less than whole-hearted. Like a tanker turning at sea, I was slow to transition from doing everything I could to prevent pregnancy to courting every opportunity to achieve it. I loved being married to Simon and wanted to wallow in that pleasure for a time. I thought I would be a good mom in a distant, far off, fantasy kind of way but now that it was a real possibility, I wasn't so sure. I was intimidated by the prospect of parenthood, although I was confident Simon would make a brilliant father: at least the kid would have that. Ruth even said, 'I think you'll make a good mother to one or two children.' It was comforting to hear, but I had to consider the source.

'No wonder your progesterone was off the charts!' the doctor congratulates me. Unbeknownst to either of us, I was already pregnant when she tested my hormone levels.

As his cells divide and conquer me, the reality of our baby fills my senses, starting with a simple line appearing on a piece of plastic to the tiny racing horse-hoof patter of his heartbeat booming through the monitor. Our emotions see-saw from elation to fear, from wonder to doubt. There are risks associated with our ages so we tell ourselves that it's enough to know that we can get pregnant; that we can try again if there is a problem. But despite these rational words, my body has already pledged full allegiance to this baby. I swell in protection around him.

I was vaguely aware of the risks of amniocentesis but my hormones fogged out much of the fear. It was only when I was flat on my back, my belly and baby exposed did I sense danger. It wasn't the foot long needle approaching my abdomen that worried me, but the toxic atmosphere filling the room. My doctor shared a practice with her husband, who was assisting in my procedure, even though it was very clear that she would have preferred to stab the needle into his eyeball at that moment.

'Is everything okay?' I ask her.

'Of course,' she says, 'everything will be fine.'

'I mean with you,' I said and wagged my finger between the two of them.

And it was fine. We watched as the needle threaded its way towards the resting baby, our breath held when he didn't initially respond, and collectively released when he eased himself away from the intrusion, a lazy, wafting hand waving at us, shooing the intrusive needle out of his lair.

Like my mother before me, I didn't need a clone myself in my own child, but I did want more people like my husband in the world. It is impossible to say with any certainty how far I would have gone to have our own child if I had not so readily become pregnant. This first flesh and blood of our own and of my own.

'Our baby will be my first blood-relative,' I say.

'That you know of,' corrected Simon.

'Yes, but that is the point, that I will *know* him or her and I'm going to be their mama!'

I wanted to see Ruth's face when I told her that I was pregnant. She had enquired about baby plans since our marriage two years before but she hadn't pushed. I knew she would be thrilled. But our family reunion to commemorate my father's 75th birthday was over a month away and even though we would be face-to-face I couldn't tell my mother then, because Irmgard would be along for the ride.

My mother rightly or wrongly had taken Irmgard Muller, a fellow resident at their assisted-living facility, Carol Woods, and an Auschwitz survivor, on as a project. This approach on my mother's part to their relationship didn't bring out the best in either of them but they persisted regardless until death did them part. My father not only didn't share my mother's complicated feelings for Irmgard, but he and Irmgard engaged in a mutual antipathy on a subdued, for my mother's sake, scale. That Ruth proceeded to appoint my father as Irmgard's sole chauffeur only added to their aversion for one another. My father, who considered his driving beyond reproach would bridle when, at the first drop of rain, Irmgard, buttressed atop her personal cushion in the back seat, would croak, 'Should we pull over?'

Irmgard, as a resident of long-standing, was widely known, if not universally popular, at Carol Woods. Although she softened in later old age, she was strongly willed, with exacting aesthetic standards. She was both uncompromising and easily offended, which made her uneasy company for some. She was also extremely interested in people and possessed a somewhat devilish sense of humour.

Born in 1920 in Halle an der Saale, she enjoyed a privileged childhood until Hitler came to power. Her parents sent her brother away to Italy, from where he made his way to safety in America and served in the American army as an enemy alien soldier. By way of safe-guarding Irmgard's future survival, she was trained as both a bookkeeper and a seamstress in Berlin. After Kristallnacht and the closure of the school, she was 'called up' and sent first to a forced labour camp and then, on April 20,1943, she was put on a train to Auschwitz as part of Joseph Goebbels' promise to make Berlin *judenfrei* (free of Jews) in time for Hitler's fifty-fourth birthday.

Forced on a death march by the SS commanders evacuating the camp in an attempt to outrun the encroaching Red Army, Irmgard and some friends escaped by jumping into a roadside ditch in a pitch-black gap between tracer fire lighting up the night sky. They fortuitously found a farmer who gave them some potatoes and let them sleep in his barn in the hopes that the liberators would look favourably upon his charity. With the aid of the Allied Forces, she fled Germany to Sweden and from there made her way to some relatives in New York who discouraged her from ever speaking about her experiences. Her Auschwitz tattoo with the number 41965 and a Star of David were a source of unwanted attention in her new life and so she was forced to have it surgically removed by those same relatives. All that remained was a black triangle from the top of the star.

Ruth was determined that Irmgard be heard and seen and her experience validated and no need was too big or too trivial for her to attempt to fulfil. This almost devotional pedestal upon which my mother placed Irmgard made for an awkward perch.

Soon after Simon and I became engaged, we visited my parents. After admiring my out-sized aquamarine engagement ring at the airport, my mother said, 'Don't show the ring to Irmgard or mention the engagement. She always wanted to get married.' She then ran through the weekend's schedule and, with the exception of the final morning, all activities included Irmgard.

With no subtle way to ask without hinting at or outright revealing my pregnancy, I hazarded a guess that if a mere engagement was unmentionable, pregnancy would be downright offensive. With this in mind, I decided to break the news over the phone for fear, not of making Irmgard uncomfortable, but of making my mother uncomfortable on Irmgard's behalf.

'Hold on, I'll get your mother,' my father said as soon as he heard my voice.

'Okay, but stay on the phone, I have some news.'

'Mom, you're going to be a grandmother again,' I say over the crackle of the speaker phone. I could picture my mother sitting on the bed cross-legged, leaning over the phone, her face in her hands, beaming 'Oh, Donna, that's wonderful news!' I basked in their joy and the joy of telling them.

'I wanted to tell you down at the reunion, but I was worried how Irmgard might react.'

'Oh, that's no problem, she loves babies,' she said blithely unaware of the turmoil I had put myself through.

I had experienced only a tiny taste of the judgement and pressure that my mother was likely subjected to at the hands of the medical professionals when she first tried to get pregnant. In my case, the push for intervention was steep and aggressive, which I adroitly sidestepped by already being pregnant. My mother had opted out of any intervention. I do not know if Ruth ever became pregnant, the professed 'conception problems' weren't specific, but she did imply that conception rather than miscarriage was the source of the difficulty. Neither she nor my father ever elaborated further.

I was too wrapped up in my own pregnancy at the time to spare a thought for my birth mother and her pregnancy with me. Looking back, I wonder how she felt when she saw the signs: the missed period, the familiar bloating, the swelling and ache of her full breasts. Did she think, 'here we go again?' and when the nausea tapered off and the happy hormones flooded in, did she dread or did she dream?

Mine was the first pregnancy that Ruth was engaged in from first to last. My sister had been living abroad when she had her children and my brother's wife had family of her own to share with. Ruth took her vicarious role very seriously indeed.

My pilates partner, mother of two, had a bumper crop of baby books which she donated to me: sixteen pregnancy books. Sixteen! I couldn't understand why I needed one manual let alone sixteen. As far as I was concerned, Simon and I had performed our respective roles and all that remained for me to do was eat enough for two and sit around waiting for the baby to show up, the way it has always happened since time immemorial. I sent half the books to my mother, but she rejected the lot:

'They're all about what could go wrong, I want to know what's happening.' So she went off to the library, as was her habit, to check out her own books. Meanwhile, Simon emailed her updates charting the baby's growth and progress each week.

We met for the family reunion at Trinity Center, in Salter Path in the Outer Banks, the barrier islands off the coast of

North Carolina. As the first order of business, Lew handed out t-shirts he'd had made for the occasion. They were grey with a large blue star in the centre, above which it said: A Star is Born and below was my father's birth date, June 28, 1928. Irmgard wore hers just once and it is the only time I ever saw her in short sleeves.

The barrier islands are already some way out into the open ocean in waters known colloquially as the Graveyard of the Atlantic. The ever-shifting sandbars of the Diamond Shoals have claimed thousands of ships and their crews and the seabed is littered with the wrecks. On days when the warning red flag forbade us from swimming we could see the riptides, distinctive runnels, like seams, in the white surf.

As soon as the flags changed to green or yellow, my sister and I plunged into the ocean. I loved being in the water, and pregnant, I felt connected with a sea inside me, buoyed and brave, embraced by a crushing force, immense and unimaginable, like time.

Dad only got as far as the covered patio at the top of the dunes, but Mom and Irmgard braved the descent. Irmgard sat on the beach, her legs splayed like a little girl's, running her fingers through the surf as the waves washed away the sand beneath her.

Leah and I held Mom between us and guided her beyond the breakers to the deeper water where we leapt up and rode the waves. She was trusting but incompetent, too slow to meet the wave and so she was caught time and again by a salty slap in the ear of her averted face. We tried to get her to jump earlier and earlier but she couldn't find the rhythm.

Like Ruth, I was put off by the fear surrounding a lot of pregnancy and birth information. I was inclined towards natural childbirth and so when we found an accelerated natural childbirth class it seemed like the right fit. While I was at pains to avoid the medicalisation of modern-day birth in the USA, I was also a busy New Yorker with a full-time job and a social schedule.

The weekly class reinforced the general mistrust of medical intervention which was designed with the convenience of the doctors and hospitals in mind and not you or your baby. Childbirth is beautiful, we were taught, but it is also a pitched battle of wills. You must be armed with hyper-vigilance and advocates to fight your corner. Come at the birth mob-handed, bring a doula and midwife, bodies you can throw at the doctors while you give birth your way. Keep the medical machinery at bay! This is the first and most important act in your baby's life so, in the immortal words of RuPaul, don't fuck it up!

The sole focus of the course was the act of delivery and the birth to the complete exclusion of life after birth, other than breast feeding, which was, of course, mandatory. There was tremendous emphasis placed on having a birth plan to avoid the scourge of medicalisation. To this end, we were also encouraged to desist from going to the hospital until the last possible moment.

I blanched at the idea of having to take a cab into Manhattan to give birth. What if there was traffic on the bridge and I gave birth in a taxi? Or worse, the Brooklyn-Battery Tunnel!

To spare myself that particular indignity, in my third trimester, I switched to a doctor at Long Island College Hospital; it was close to our Brooklyn apartment and boasted a new birthing centre. Unfortunately, there were no midwives available around my projected due date. My new doctor walked us through the birthing process once again, revealing an alarming verbal tick. 'When you have the watchamacallit, baby, your watchamacallit, um, cervix dilates, and the baby moves into the watchamacallit, birth canal ...' She nixed the birthing centre idea. 'I don't like doing that, I like to be in control of the watchamacallit, birth at every stage.' The hospital was within walking distance so this 'plan' was better, if only marginally, than giving birth in the back of a taxi.

Back in birth class there was lip service paid to the likelihood of things not going according to plan and that bringing home a healthy baby was the most important outcome. Instead of just nodding at these words, I wish I had taken them to heart.

We devised a simple but perfectly formed strategy for the birth: I would make lasagne and rotate on my pilates ball while listening to an absorbing audio book. After my waters broke and the contractions started in earnest, I would waddle up the road to the hospital where I would almost immediately be delivered of a baby who would be named Parker if a girl and Dexter if a boy. That was the plan.

My due date was also the anniversary of the day we first met, January 15. I was happy and magnificently enormous in those final weeks of pregnancy. I loved the shape of the baby in the bath where my own bulk fell away, outlining that adorable little butt. I communed with the little being squirming through his night-time perambulations around my womb, stretching his legs and contorting inside me. I was sure I'd have a couple of weeks more to wallow in this way, a walking pool with my bathing baby inside. I was never on time, why would my baby arrive on the dot?

I didn't feel well the on the evening of the 14th. I made salmon instead of lasagne and listened to a John le Carré audio book while squatting on my ball. Is this it? Is this the beginning of labour? I felt like I should be drinking more water, but I somehow didn't manage to.

I felt better in the morning and we headed to my routine check-up. A nurse we hadn't met before undertook the scan. Without a word, she abruptly left the room. She returned with a doctor and they consulted the screen. This no longer seemed routine; a dull alarm flared up.

'You have no amniotic fluid, we have to induce the baby now,' the doctor who we also had never seen, told us. I insisted I needed to hear it from Dr Whatchamacallit, but she too confirmed that there was no, watchamacallit, amniotic fluid and they had to induce me immediately.

'I have to go home and get a bag, I'm not prepared.'

'You have an hour.'

'What if I don't come back?' I wheedled.

'Then I'll come get you.'

We crammed all the 'how to induce labour naturally' methods into the allotted hour – sex, exercise, spicy food, nipple stimulation – to no avail.

We returned to the hospital and were deposited in a windowless room and a drip was painfully inserted into a vein in my hand and a cervix ripening suppository placed in my vagina. At some point in the night, while Simon slept, the contractions began. I gripped the wall, gratefully gritting my teeth, hoping I was back on track to give birth naturally. Not wanting to wake Simon I collapsed on the toilet between contractions. When they eased off I went back to bed but was too anxious to sleep.

Morning arrived and with it my delivery nurse to bring me to the birthing room. I asked if there was time for a quick shower, that I hadn't slept and felt rotten. She turned on me, angry. 'You haven't slept? You're going to be too tired for labour.' She flinched at the sight of my bruised hand where the drip was inexpertly inserted, she reinserted it and told me to hurry up in the shower.

An inspection revealed that the suppository had been flushed out, which is why my contractions had tapered off. It wasn't all bad news, my cervix had started to dilate so they decided to wait to see if labour developed. It was pretty clear though, that the baby wasn't ready to come out. He was tucked up as high as could be on my chest. And I wasn't ready to be parted from my baby, not this way.

Labour did not progress, so they started to 'push' Pitocin into my arm to hurry the baby along. The contractions were strong and uncomfortable, I asked to move with the contractions on the ball but they wanted me on the bed. And then my water broke – the water they told me I didn't have – and with it, the baby's distress signal in the form of the meconium exited. The baby had violated the first and most important rule of hospitality and hygiene: you don't shit where you eat. Things were now incontrovertibly medicalised.

They strapped a monitor for the baby's heartbeat around my middle. During the nurse's lunch break, the monitor slipped off the baby and started charting my much slower heart beats. In the space of one inhalation of breath and the exhalation, the room flooded with a swirl of bodies and shouting. I was whipped around onto all fours and a monitor was screwed into my baby's tender unborn head. I was trussed to the hospital bed and once again the Pitocin was cranked. I lay passive, hogtied by the wires in and around me as the induced contractions rippled through me.

Strapped in and unable to move, my cervix stubbornly un-dilated, tears leaked from me as I listened to the woman in the next room pushing her baby. This was not the plan.

It had started to snow and for some reason, presumably for Martin Luther King Day, there were fireworks outside the window, across the East River lighting up lower Manhattan.

Dr Watchamacllit arrived with the shift change and recommended an anaesthetising epidural. I ascended and floated above, witnessing rather than feeling the contractions running through me like waves.

After thirty-six hours of fruitless, induced labour, we ditched the now tattered plan. In defeat, we ran up the white flag and agree to a C-section at 11:30 p.m. I was screened from the sight of my baby's birth by a sheet erected across my chest and then I heard the baby howl.

'Did we get a Parker or a Dexter?' I shouted in the direction of my toes.

'It's a Dexter!'

The doctors snatched him and hosed him off in a sink in the corner. They brought his swaddled body, completely covered except his red, screaming face to us but held him too high for me to see.

'I can't see him,' I panicked. They merely bobbed down with him and then ran off to the Neonatal ICU with Simon running after them.

Numbed by the epidural and exhaustion, I lost the sense of emergency, I didn't fully appreciate the danger of inhaling the meconium.

I dully felt the mucking out sensation of the placenta being removed. I had relinquished all control, even over my limbs, unable to push, Watchamacallit had to do it for me.

Lying there looking up at the ceiling, I remembered once hearing that women, possibly even my birth mother, who gave their babies up for adoption, were also screened from the belly down, an opaque divide between the top and bottom halves of their bodies, forced to labour blindly. They were blocked from seeing and bonding with their babies, or maybe their newborns were shielded from the taint of their fallen mothers.

I was cleaned and tucked away, left alone in limbo. Simon eventually returned with the doctors. Their upside-down faces discussed Dexter's condition as they wheeled me to a room. Still in my epidural stupor, I marvelled that this hypothetical name, our private name for a baby that was in me, was being used out in the world to signify our baby boy. He's real, he's here, is all that I heard. The import of their words was temporarily lost on me.

'Dexter has a bubble of air in his chest that is pressing on his heart, we have to put a tube in his chest.'

It would be years until I was fully alerted to the struggle he faced when he aspirated the meconium, his tiny lungs clogged with the tarry, green mess.

Simon and Leah were allowed to see Dexter before his operation. 'He's beautiful,' they enthused.

The nurse arrived to see if my colostrum had come in. 'Can Mommy pump for the baby?'

'Can Mommy see the baby?' I pleaded.

It was twelve hours, half of his first day gone, before I was allowed in to see Dexter.

I hear him before I see him. He is hollering mad, bellowing despite his mucky lungs, his clenched fists bouncing up and down in frustration in his plastic cot. He is a giant Gulliver surrounded by rows of Lilliputian premature babies with their heart-rending, twig-like limbs. I cradle Dexter, shielding him from the clarion alarms that ring out emergency throughout the ward. As I bring him to my breast, underneath the medical beepings, I can just make out the song on the radio. It's 'Thank You' by Dido.

I first heard this gloriously uplifting song as I got dressed on the morning that Simon and I were married. And finally, just to be with Dexter was indeed having the best day of my life.

7

TO GRANDMOTHER'S HOUSE WE GO (2005)

The sickening thud of Dexter's peachy skull hitting the wood floor was followed by a terrifying silence as I scrambled back to the bedroom where I had left him momentarily unattended on the bed, cardinal parenting sin number one. Relief curdled into nausea and a different level of panic as his howls erupted. An inauspicious start to our first trip away from home but all in all, a pretty average morning. I was not winning at motherhood.

No sooner had the epidural worn off than I was dragged out to sea on a riptide of panic which abated only when Dexter slept. In those rare moments, the adrenaline subsided and a rush of almost orgasmic love engulfed me.

I hate not sleeping even for a night. It immediately upends my emotional balance. To not sleep for days and weeks and months, to wake after two hours with a headache like a tumour, my soul empty and hollow and hopeless was ruinously crushing. The dark sleepless nights seeped into my heart. Dexter's wee smiles perked me up but couldn't prop me up. I sat silently screaming and held my head away so that my tears wouldn't splash onto his downy, tufted head, promising him and myself that tomorrow I would be better. The endless fear turned to acidic poison and I was wrathful.

Yes, my mother and I have repaired our relationship, yes, we are close, but yes damage has been done. I was now returned to that helpless state that I was in as a child with nothing to draw on but the fear of those long-gone days. And the sustained panic of my childhood that I have papered over but not resolved has distilled into anger with age, a volcano of molten rage that erupts at all that is out of my control in the face of this new moment of childhood. But this time, I am the mother.

Four months of flailing and floundering in the treacherous sea of new motherhood and I have just started to find my feet. Exhausted, I stagger forward, the flotsam and jetsam of my former life strewn about me.

In my own medieval map of motherhood, dragons and sea monsters are placed over the yawning maw of unknowns. Each day is a maiden voyage through uncharted territory and the monsters rear up at the slightest fluctuation. There is one heavenly morning when Dexter and I fall asleep just after he's nursed, sleeping nose to tiny nose; on another he is pure bliss in his first fit of laughing. And at last, a baby sling has given sleepy succour to Dexter and finally returned my arms to me during the day; nights now occasionally stretch to a blissful five hours of blanketing sleep.

I wonder how my mother did this with three of us. I wonder how my birth mother could have missed it, this crushing love.

The morning Dexter's head hit the floor is also the day we were headed to Chapel Hill, North Carolina to visit my parents. Not once have I left the house with everything I need for lunch, let alone seven days away from our Brooklyn nest. With my 'working memory' still enjoying an extended maternity leave I put my faith in lists. Lists are extremely effective *aide memoires* but they work best if you remember to look at them. Two blocks into the cab ride and my memory resurfaced: 'I forgot the formula!' I shouted.

The anger behind the stress and anxiety of being a parent is derived from my childhood but not directed at my parents. My mother called each night to check-in or check up on me. 'Okay, what's happening?' was her standard opening line. The calls were a little lifeline each day, similar to the moment when Simon stepped through the door after work. I wasn't alone.

Mom and Dad came to visit in February, spreading the drive from North Carolina over two days. They avoided my sister's house in Westchester because her children were sick and chose instead to stay at the Ramada Plaza Hotel at LaGuardia Airport in Queens on the grounds that it was closer to my father's family cemetery, smack dab in the middle of Nowhere, Long Island. 'We have a great view of Shea Stadium from the motel,' Dad boasted, 'but the traffic is terrible.'

'The people are so rude,' my mother added.

I saw them from our living room window as they picked carefully through the snow, they looked bleached in their matching anoraks. Their faces, loose with age, unfolded with delight at the sight of Dexter. They opened and softened as they bent over him; their eyes wide with joy.

Magi like, they came bearing gifts for the boy. For the parents, they brought a large bag of foodstuffs. I peered into the bag and lifted out one of two packs of fancy cheese biscuits, 'those were only recently opened,' my mother said.

There were also lemon biscuits (opened), potato chips, grissini (several packs from their dining hall), fortune cookies, various pieces of fruit, three Southern-style breakfast biscuits wrapped in napkins from breakfast the morning they left North Carolina and a package of McDonald's french fries carefully folded over to contain the eight remaining fries within. Leah, who was visiting, and I convulsed with laughter upon seeing the fries. Simon was convinced that the fries were put in the bag accidentally, but we knew better.

I eased into the balmy warmth of North Carolina and the unhurried pace at my parents' where life glides by on one smooth level. Whether Dexter's calm sleeping relaxed me or perhaps because I was less fraught, he slept – I didn't care, I was just grateful that there was a place on earth where we could both slumber in peace. Tending to Dexter was our only obligation; no emails, no cooking, no cleaning or phoning or keeping up with life. The days were generally organised around precisely timed meals. Breakfast was eaten at home and only one meal a day at the dining hall because, as my father declared after an alarming and offensive bout of indigestion: 'Never two buffets in one day.'

The raised, round bull's-eye of a bruise front and centre on Dexter's forehead was my own mark of Cain. Once word got out that there was a baby on campus, we were beset at the dining hall, surrounded on all sides by twinkly-eyed Ruth Gordon look-alikes, their veined hands grasping for Dexter, showering him with coos and oohs and ahs.

As my mother predicted, Irmgard's welcome was warmest of all. He laughed and gurgled on her bouncing knees as she crooned a gentle version of 'Hoppe, Hoppe, Reiter', evoked from her own childhood. With her glittering blue eyes hugely magnified by her glasses and her goblin's grin she bore an uncanny resemblance to Gollum reunited with his 'Precious'.

As we sat down to our first dinner of the visit, Dad blithely commented, 'I don't think anyone wants those cemetery plots. I've asked everybody in the family.'

A few weeks back, during one of my mother's daily calls, my father had piped up over the speaker phone asking if I had any interest in a pair of the Long Island cemetery plots he had been given by his uncle, Larry, one of his father's seven siblings. I immediately declined with a 'thanks, no thanks', to which my father said, 'think about it.' I now felt compelled to ask:

'Why don't you want them?'

Halfway between the dining table and the kitchen hatch, my mother's head whips around. 'I'm not going back to New York!' she blurts out with a snort.

'The traffic's terrible!' says Dad.

Life at my parents' house had a leisurely rhythm. Dexter and my father forged a bond that is more like a Vulcan mind meld. They are the same person at different ends of the life-spectrum, before-and-after pictures with identical outsized heads and sky-blue eyes. They were content to goo and gah together in perfect harmony. My mother had cleared her schedule, temporarily suspending her social whirl of gardening club, book club, Latin class, bocce, ping-pong and croquet for the duration of our visit, with one notable exception.

'On Sunday, I have a recorder recital,' she announced and then quickly backtracked, 'it's not an official concert; it's really just for us and another group to play for each other. But, you're welcome to come.'

My father chimed in with, 'Paddington wants to go; he always listens to you practise but he never gets to go to the concert.'

The Paddington my father referred to was the bear of Michael Bond's imagination; this iteration stood roughly one-and-a-half feet tall in his red patent Wellington boots. Dad acquired him with Macy's vouchers, which were a Christmas gift from someone at work, in 1980. I was in eighth grade when our new family member arrived; I spotted the bear, lying on his back, peeping out of a shiny red Macy's bag in the backseat when my father picked me up from my cello lesson one night. I thought the 'Please look after this bear' instruction on the tag around his neck might be directed at me as I was the only child left in the house, but, by that time, I can guarantee you that unless that bear had been sporting Gloria Vanderbilt jeans I could somehow have squeezed into, I had lost my love of stuffed animals. I needn't have worried; he was a gift for my mother.

We were not a family given to ostentatious present buying. Hanukkah with its eight nights of presents was that magical time of year when we'd receive our annual supply of socks and underwear. My mother faithfully re-enacted the miracle of the long-burning oil, making a present that should last for just one night, last two: one night your comics-wrapped bundle would reveal a pyjama top, the next night, the bottoms. On birthdays we received more frivolous offerings, a Frisbee or a yoyo.

For our part, we only ever gave our parents IOUs. We hoarded boxes in the run-up to Mother's Day and then reverently placed the scrap of paper – redeemable for a future present – into a plastic capsule salvaged from a cereal box prize, like it needed to be preserved for posterity and dug up at a time when we would be capable of fulfilling the promise. We buried the capsule in box after box, wrapping each one in comics, the successive boxes intended to convey the weight of our appreciation. We laughed riotously at our joke when she came up with box after box.

But on the odd occasion, my father would buck the trend and indulge in expensive hobby-related gadgets for himself. An enlarger for the dark room he created in one of the windowless closets of my sister's room. A Hewlett Packard programmable, scientific calculator to track his running – an early do-it-yourself Fitbit. He was a pioneer of the home gym, installing a treadmill in the basement when his burgeoning fears of swan attacks along the river path and turned ankles put him off running outdoors. This was no flimsy conveyor belt affair, but the identical model used in doctor's offices at the time to perform electrocardiogram tests. He would emerge from the basement, dripping with sweat and announce, 'I stink therefore I am.'

He also made a few grand gestures for my thrifty mother that improbably managed to capture the whimsy of romance combined with strategic practicality. When the local tennis courts were vandalised, my father presented my mother with her very own tennis net. We would march, *en famille*, to the courts on Sunday mornings, net and broom in hand and while we swept the court free of broken bottles and cigarette butts, Dad would unfurl the net along the pockmarked court. Once attached we tightened either end to his precise calibrations; he carefully adjusted the net to match his racket's exact height plus its width while Mom looked on with smug approval.

But Paddington, despite serving no practical purpose, was an even greater gift than the tennis net; he was a total ace.

I have no recollection of my own homecoming but I can only hope there was as much fanfare as greeted Paddington. He was my parents' final and most successful adoption; he was by far the best-behaved and most loyal of their children and he bore stoic witness as they moved into the empty-nested phase of their lives.

Paddington became a medium of emotional parley for my father. If, for instance, he stopped on his way back from exchanging CDs and books at the library to pick up a milkshake and fries for two, he would say: 'Paddington thought you might want a treat.' It was Paddington, wearing one of our outgrown and discoloured White Plains Recreation Day Camp t-shirts, who wished my mother 'Happy Birthday' and 'Happy Anniversary,' each February, he was her tender, devoted valentine, her courtly troubadour.

Mom and Dad were both passionate about music and both equally devoid of the merest vestige of natural musicality. My father kindly restricted himself to playing the radio or stereo quite loud, checking out records and CDs from the library, brazenly taping them and then storing them in countless boxes, each carefully catalogued and cross-referenced by composer and musician.

My mother, on the other hand, was more pro-active and conducted her own music appreciation class for our benefit. Our music tuition began with the song flute and graduated to the recorder. She started Paul on Suzuki method violin lessons at age six. Our local elementary school loaned musical instruments to students when they reached the fourth grade, so my mother played a recording of *Peter and the Wolf* to help us choose an instrument. My sister picked the loping cat, played by the clarinet. When it was my turn, I liked the trilling bird, represented by the flute. I don't know why my mother vetoed my first choice. Too girly perhaps? Too blonde? Too waspy? Maybe she thought another stringed instrument would make a better family trio. I ignored Paul's recommendation of the violin – 'I can give you lessons,' he enthused – and instead opted for the cello.

My mother herself stuck resolutely with the recorder despite having zero talent and being beyond awful. I don't know when she first tackled the instrument of our torture but she 'played' the recorder as long as I can remember and practised religiously. The supposedly universal 10,000-hour 'rule to expertise' espoused by K. Anders Ericsson and popularised by Malcolm Gladwell did not apply to my mother. What she called practising could hardly be described as 'deliberate practising to augment natural talent,' at least not with a straight face. I once asked Leah why Mom was so very bad considering how much she practised. 'She isn't practising, she's just repeating herself!' Leah said.

When my mother wasn't employed outside the home, we didn't have keys to the basement and were forced to wait at the front door until she was good and ready to relinquish her contented solitude and let us into the house after school. She would practise, deliberately blocking us out and refusing to answer our repeated pressing on the doorbell. Locked out, we would stand directly beneath her bedroom window while she sat on the bed tunelessly hooting.

The day before the recital-which-was-not-a-real-recital I sat with Mom on her bed reviewing the music they'd be playing at the non-concert. She confessed to being a bit nervous. 'I never know when to come in on this one; it starts with forty rests!' she said.

'Do you count the rests?'

'No,' she said with a gleeful smile.

On Sunday, she got a ride to the hall early with another member of the ensemble. Simon declined my mother's offer of attending the non-recital in favour of staying home with Dexter. As Dad and I headed out to the car he repeated the same plaintive line, 'Paddington really wants to go to the concert. He always gets to hear her practise, but he never gets to go to the concerts.' I thought he might prefer Paddington and his faux fur ears to go in his own place for once.

'Well, if it's any consolation, it's not a real concert,' I said.

He then put one of his over-sized, battered and taped up briefcases into the back of the car. 'What's in the bag? I asked.

'It's a secret.' I knew not to ask again. If my father said it's a secret, nothing would loosen his lips, likewise a private joke; it stayed private. I doubt he would even whisper it to Paddington.

We arrived during the rehearsal and found seats in my mother's sight line. There was already a thin smattering of audience members, all clearly family like us and here under sufferance, questioning half-smiles on their faces which were swiftly replaced by grimaces as the twenty-five recorders screeched into a deafening cacophony that I could only recognise as *Greensleeves* after the third time through.

There is no discernible difference between the rehearsal and the actual concert save the tap of the baton by the conductor, who delivered the same expectation-lowering speech Mom gave us: 'This isn't an official recital but we're glad you're here.'

At the first note, Dad leaned down and opened the briefcase. Stuffed inside, feet and furry paws thrust upwards in front of his squashed head, lay Paddington. Dad flattened open the flaps with care and reached in to untuck Paddington's baseball cap and then placed it carefully on his own head. The bear's original red felt sou'wester had long since disintegrated.

'This way she'll know Paddington is here,' he explained matter-of-factly.

'Oh, is that his hat?' I whispered back.

'No, it's mine, but I let him wear it.'

I couldn't tell whether Mom came in after the forty rests or launched in too early or too late but she didn't seem to do any worse than anyone else. Dad and I nudged each other and nodded when she looked our way and we think she clocked the cap. While the rest of the audience sat shell-shocked and blinking in bafflement at the discordant din, Dad and I were giddy and grinning, flushed with conspiratorial anticipation.

Dad scooted back to the car after the concert and propped Paddington up on Mom's seat.

'Oh,' she exclaimed, hands across her heart, 'Paddington was there?' Her voice was high with surprise and warm with pleasure. 'He always gets to hear me practise but he never gets to go to the concert,' she shook her head, marvelling.

'Dad was wearing his hat; I thought you knew he was there,' I said.

'I saw the hat, but I thought it was symbolic,' she said. She sat Paddington on her lap for the drive home, alternately resting her chin on his matted head or patting it, the hat having been returned to its rightful owner.

On the morning of our wedding, my mother told me that she'd prepared 'a few words' and I throbbed with quiet joy, an added boon to the day. After lunch she stood: 'I have a few words I want to say to Donna. If the rest of you can hear me, fine, but as I say, these words are for Donna.' With that, she turned her back to the guests and addressed herself to me.

'Donna, a marriage doesn't happen on a particular day or place. A marriage is built through the months and years of laughter, toil, understanding, confusion, adventure and forgiveness. Later, if you are lucky and devoted, you will find an even richer, deeper love; a love that is a marriage.'

She didn't mention Paddington, but he is the stuffed embodiment of their bond.

*

Instead of packing to go back to Brooklyn, I sat with Mom on the bed going through her mother's jewellery. Ruth never wore much jewellery and was furious when I pierced my own ears with two pieces of ice, a needle and thread. She no longer wore her wedding ring. She handed over the gold Tiffany's cuff we bought Nana after she and Papa had been burgled, still in its faded pouch and box. She swung one of Nana's gold pendants back and forth like a hypnotist, 'I'm not ready to give this one up yet. I don't know why.' We smiled and shrugged our shoulders at each other over the necklace. She also gave me two travel clocks, my Yiddish workbooks, my elementary school report cards, some essays from high school, an ice bucket in the shape of an owl and a spaghetti fork.

'Will you come visit?' I didn't dare look at her face.

'We'll see,' she said, still fiddling with the necklace. 'We'll see' was then, and had always been, a deferred 'Hell no.'

I sobbed on the plane home. 'I don't know when I'll see them again,' I snuffled. When I had announced that I was pregnant to my parents, Ruth had asked shyly, 'does this change your plans to move to London?' It hadn't and what had been only a vague plan to move back 'at some point' to Simon's native England had hardened into our July 18, 2005 departure, a few months away.

'We're moving to London, not Mars; we'll be back to visit,' Simon soothed me.

'It was a really lovely visit,' Mom said when our daily calls resumed the next day. 'It was, it really was, Mom,' I agreed.

A fortnight later, I swung up our stoop in the May sunshine. I set down the heavy shopping bags, looped my arm across Dexter, sleeping peacefully nestled in his sling, and pressed play on the blinking answering machine.

'Uh, this is Dad. Your mother . . . your mother had a bad thing. An aneurysm burst. She's in surgery now; it's going to be eight hours. I'll call you when it's over. This is a very serious thing.'

I listened to the message again before I called back, but to reach Dad's message I had to scroll through the six saved messages already there. Each one was my mother playing 'Happy Birthday' to me on the recorder, each rendition with a different note out of tune. No words, just the recorder and the bent note, just for me. One for every year we have owned this phone.

8

LIKE A FISH (2005)

The answering machine clicked off, sealing me into a static electricity bubble of white noise.

Moments prior, I had been swinging through the dappled May sunshine, brimming with happiness and anticipation as I rushed to meet a dear friend at our door.

Instead of Sara, I am met with my father's message and then nothing but a snap and crackle in my head, synapses sputtering and guttering into a long hiss.

And then I was roused by Dexter's squirming and gurgling. I summoned Simon home from work as Dexter's fist crawled over my swollen breasts. Swaddled in my faux-denim breast pillow, I sat on the bed and called my uncle, sister and brother. The calls ping-ponged across our distances, echoing each other's cries of 'Oh my god!' and 'She can't, she just can't' over Dexter's suckling head. We waited, suspended in dread, for my father to call after Mom's surgery. At the hospital, wrapped in his own blanket of fear, Dad seemed just as inaccessible as Mom did.

We are a streamlined and compact family, and had not yet

faced the prospect of a death that would devastate all of us so equally. We had been systematically shielded from death and illness from an early age, death and dying was the grown-ups' business. Death had visited but it hadn't punched us in the guts just yet.

My first profound loss of life was the green tiger barb. It was the only cool fish out of the eleven tanks of tropical fish that dominated our living room. The red oscars were okay; they were so big that Uncle Lew threatened to sauté them for an appetiser every time he came to visit. They sometimes flopped out of the tank and lay sawing from side to side on the carpeted floor.

The tiger barb's blood was on my hands. All the fish, dead or alive, were my fault. One rash, rebellious toss of the ping pong at the school fair wrought a litany of death by ick, skin and gill flukes, hole-in-the-head and finally by cat.

Our school fair was like any other elementary school fair and we were encouraged to spend our nickels, dimes and pennies on fund-raising activities like the cake walk, or splatter paintings made on revolving record disks. After the cake walk, the next biggest money spinner due to the sheer volume of punters, was the ping pong toss. There was a strict moratorium on the game in our house. The prize was a goldfish and we were not pet people. My brother once had either a turtle or turtles and it or they developed shell rot or soft shell and died. No more pets.

I swaggered into the fair, unsupervised, with the knowledge that I was the final Freed to darken the fair's door. I was twelve and in sixth grade and I would be history after graduation the very next week. I stepped up to the ping pong stand with cavalier abandon. I tossed and I won.

The tank frothed with orange fish, but one stood out from the school; he had a black stripe from the top of his head to his tail. 'That one, that's the one I want!' I said when the carny tried to bag me a run of the mill orange blob. The wily fish eluded the net three times but if I was going to get in trouble for a damn fish, it had better be the one I wanted. His name was Spike and I loved him instantly – my first bad boy crush.

I sauntered home, Spike spinning in his plastic bag, and pushed him forward as casually as I could. To my great surprise, my father poured him into a vase, grabbed my sister and sped off to the pet store for a tank, filter, heater, pH balancer and more fish, guppies and the like. I stayed home and communed with Spike, who was enjoying being away from the swarm of orange, basking in his freedom, loving the solo life even as the unfiltered tap water slowed him down. It was his lone-wolf heart which first attracted him to me and was to be his downfall.

Dad got the new tank up and running and as soon as the pump bubbled to life, we poured Spike into his new home. And then the mob of other fish plopped in. This did not go down well. Spike went to work systematically attacking the other fish while they mindlessly plucked gravel and inanely chased trails of poop. I was outraged when it was Spike who was ejected and returned to the fish store instead of the gormless interlopers. I promptly lost all interest in the workaday fish that replaced my Spike. Until the green tiger barb.

The fish collection expanded to cover two walls of the living room. Four huge tanks flanked the stereo cabinet and two other stacks of four tanks each stood against the adjacent wall. To my father, they were a collection, like his cowrie shells and his stamps from the Philippines and Guam or his collection of first day covers. Mom liked to come in from work, pull up a chair and lose herself in their fluid swooping and diving.

Two years after the fish proliferation, Cat arrived. It was

Thanksgiving and it was my mother who fed her. I wouldn't have been that bold. But the cat stuck around and she was lovely and little and mostly white with calico patches. I fell hard for her and was elated that I had the honour of naming her. She made her purring way inside the house.

Whenever Cat ventured into the living room I stood guard over the tiger barb tank, which was the only one within her reach. She seemed as entranced by the tiger barb's flashing emerald flanks as he darted around the tank as I was. Every day when I opened the door after school, I was greeted by Cat standing stock still, one foot on the shelf where the tiger barb tank stood, the other front leg held over the tank, paw poised to hook a fish.

The inevitable occurred and of course she ate the one green tiger barb, not any of the ten silver ones or other anodyne fish that roamed that tank, nope, she ate the only interesting fish in the entire shoal. And that was the end of Cat; she was returned to the wilds of our neighbourhood from whence she came. I howled with the unfairness of it.

When she was still loitering around the property the next day, I resolved that if she wasn't allowed in the house, I wasn't stepping foot in it either. It was January and cold. Around the three-hour mark of my protest on the front porch, when my commitment to defending the cat's rights battled with my frozen feet, Dad opened the door and announced that Cat could stay but only in the basement.

Around the same time as the green tiger barb's demise, a boy in our neighbourhood was struck by a car and killed. Days before, I had seen him standing between the back seats of our school bus, waving at his father who was driving up behind the bus, a beatific smile lighting up his sweet face. We heard his family held an open-casket wake and that his mother preserved his room the way it was the day he died.

My brother was home from college at the start of that same summer and I overheard him complaining to Mom: 'What kind of letter was that? It only had one line: Great Aunt Kate died?'

'It also had a cheque,' my mother said.

I was at camp the summer my mother's best friend Marlene died from cancer. All I knew was that she was sick when I left for camp. I asked how she was when I came home eight weeks later. 'Uh, she died.' Ruth's attempt at breezy dismissal was belied by her reddened eyes. She looked crushed by Marlene's death.

When I caught up with my parents just before the Vassar College commencement ceremony when I graduated with the class of 1989, my mother looked harassed and preoccupied. She had just shut her friend Judy's hand in the car door. On top of that, she said, she had some bad news to tell me but it would have to wait until after the ceremony. Charlie Gibson, who was the last-minute replacement commencement-speaker for Ted Koppel, spoke about how he, one half of the presenting team on *Good Morning America*, would rather employ candidates with a liberal arts background than anyone who had majored in communications. Little did I know that I would end up working at *Good Morning America* a year later. My mind had been catapulted into overdrive by my mother's attention-grabbing suggestion of impending doom and all I could think was, who has cancer?

To my great relief, my mother reported that it was Grandma Lily who had passed away. Lily was our step grand-mother who had stopped sending me any birthday presents when I was six because my brother and sister didn't write 'thank you' cards. She had an unmistakable, high, nasal voice.

'Helllllllooooooo?'

'Hi Grandma Lily,' I bellowed back when she called.

'Do you know who this is?' the formulaic pantomime would invariably continue.

I was expecting to stay at school to celebrate with friends and hadn't even started packing but as the funeral was only a few days away, we shoved all my belongings into plastic bags and set off directly for Miami, Florida.

All the way down the Eastern Seaboard, my father sat at the helm with Mom riding shotgun while I lolled on the back seat surrounded by pillows. As we sailed south on I95, we listened to cassette after cassette of Michael Dobb's *House of Cards*. I lost myself in the story of political intrigue at the very heart of British politics. Each day, when my mother, who was not a good traveller, had her fill of the car, we pulled off the highway at the first motel with a pool.

'Every wedding, I mean funeral, brings up the last one,' my mother said as we bobbed in the pool in the setting sun, highlighting another frequent phenomenon: the interchanging of the words for the two events that bring whole families together.

At the end of the synagogue service, before the burial, the rabbi announced that shiva would be observed at two different apartments in the same North Miami Beach building, one at my grandfather's, the widower, and one at his sister-in-law Belle's, his sworn enemy owing to the Ugly Remote Control Incident of 1982.

Grandpa Aaron's most notable characteristic other than his wandering hands, was his epic ability to form deep-seated and irrational feuds; his longest and most futile was with one of his brothers whom he bitterly resented for not leaving him anything in his will; it was Aaron who found him when he'd died. 'That ingrate! How could he not know I was going to find him? Who else was going to look?'

The beginning of each visit with him was hallmarked by

a catalogue of sins committed against him and an exhaustive list of who was in and who was out. Are we talking to Hilde? Yeah, she's okay. Are we talking to ... No! Over *his* dead body!

Graveside, Belle catapulted out of her seat to be the first to throw soil to cover the coffin; her fistful would sanctify Lily before Aaron's rotten handful of dirt besmirched her. Grandpa Aaron sat in state in the living room of his apartment, surrounded by the cigar boxes, glass jars and vases that he bedecked with cowrie shells, some of which he had decorated with bubbly eyes and red, nail-polished mouths. Braced in his armchair and resembling the homing pigeons he used to keep on his Brooklyn rooftop, he glared at the guests who stopped by to pay their respects. 'It's one of her spies,' he'd say, as each mourner left who either came from Belle's or was headed there, 'she's woiss than a dawg!' This was snarled in his old school, contorted Brooklyn accent by way of the Garment District. He pronounced 'thirty-third and third' as 'toidy toid and toid'.

'He'll drop dead the day he forgives the last person,' my father said. Aaron would live to ninety-six, pinching asses and cursing family to the last bitter minute. Years later when Dad was in his late eighties he would tell me, 'I don't know where my father is buried and I don't care.' He had blocked out the plots in Long Island and only remembered his father's selfishness when it came to his first wife, Hannah, Dad's mother. Suffering from breast cancer, his mother had sat on the beach at Coney Island with her children while Aaron 'cavorted', in my father's words, with his girlfriend. When Dad's uncles called Aaron out on this, his response was, 'it's too painful for her to have sex, what do you want me to do?' Hannah died when Dad was twenty-five.

Aunt June, my father's older sister, flagged under the parade of shiva visitors and Aaron's spiteful bitching. Mom suggested I accompany June on a few rounds of the connecting balcony overlooking the pool in the centre of the courtyard. 'Our mother's unveiling was awful. It was just me, your father and Aaron so not enough people to say the kaddish, and we didn't know any of the prayers so some guy came to pray with us and he carried on so; it was just terrible.' In the car on the way back to New York, my father vividly corroborated June's story, 'there was a rent-a-rabbi who roamed the cemetery to say the prayers for you and he started dancing on my mother's grave, it was terrible.' My mother turned to me with an I-told-you-so look.

In August of that same summer after Lily's funeral, my parents escorted me to Boston to look after Nana. She had broken her arm and I was detailed to do the cooking, cleaning and general looking after her and Papa until my brother's wedding a few weeks later.

In the years before we attended sleep-away camps for the whole of the summer, we were sent to Nana and Papa's for a week. A few times Leah and I made the journey by bus on our own. Nana was a strict and authoritarian housekeeper, but there was something looser about her than my mother. She had no hidden corners, no dark areas and undercurrents. Her judgements were harsh but predictable. It was also clear she loved us and loved having us there.

It was Nana who taught us table manners, again, harsh and inflexible at the time, but I was grateful for some guidance for when I went to other people's homes who did not eat with their fingers and lick their plates clean. She, very unlike her daughter, also saw value in being well-dressed and presentable. The summer before my junior year of high school, she bought me a pair of grey, pointy-toed flats with a stylish twist of leather across the toes. I wore them even when I abraded the pads of my feet through the holes in their ragged soles.

I spent many of my college vacations at Nana and Papa's. I joked to my university friends that while they jetted off to Jamaica for Spring Break, I headed to Jamaica Plain, Massachusetts and while they partied all night, I pulled all-nighters gossiping with my grandmother. (The parallel universe in which I would ask my mother for money to go to Jamaica for Spring Break does not and never did exist; as it was, I worked two campus jobs to pay for my books.) Nana regaled me with stories of her youthful hi-jinks. She grew up in Boston, one of six children of Russian immigrants. Her mother, determined that her five daughters should marry well, studied the dresses in Filene's windows and then hurried home to replicate them – without a pattern – for her girls. Nana, named Esther but called Esta, collected silver spoons as trophies from her dates. On one occasion, the bill came listing the two coffees and one silver spoon, which the young man sat opposite her paid without comment. I still have this motley collection of pilfered silver mementos in my kitchen drawer. It's too late to ask her if the one from the Harvard Union was from her first date with Papa, Sawyer Bolanski as he was to her then.

I spent the weeks running up to Paul and Rachel's wedding at my grandparents' apartment, talking, baking, cooking and smoking. 'Papa thinks you're a brilliant cook. See? So there,' she said, sitting at the tiny kitchen table while I reproduced recipes under her close supervision. When we got to the wedding, she didn't want my help; she shooed me away with the instructions 'make sure your mother looks presentable.'

I braided Mom's hair into a tidy French plait and applied light makeup around her eyes. I pointed out the run in her tights, she nodded but didn't change them. She looked pretty in a floral purple dress picked up from a thrift store. I was also wearing a '60s thrift store find, abstract floral in emerald green with bright red shoes. 'Her hair's too tight,' Nana hissed at me.

After the wedding I returned to Nana and Papa's to settle them back in. As soon as her arm was healed, Nana was scheduled for a major hip operation so she was thrilled to have witnessed the wedding. 'Rachel looked lovely,' she gushed. 'Everyone said Ruth looked nice,' I added. 'Yes, they were surprised,' she griped sourly. 'They wouldn't have remarked on it if it was a normal event. See? So there,' which was Nana's signature summation, apropos of everything and nothing at all and usually accentuated with a pointed, mauve-painted nail against the table, a cigarette in the other hand.

The hip operation was not a success, but the patient didn't die. Nana was left paralysed and vulnerable from an open wound in her back. Before I went in to see her, Uncle Lew stayed me with, 'you won't recognise her,' shock and pain in his own face. And she was reduced, left with ragdoll limbs, her head comparatively giant, her hair, which had always been washed and set weekly, was disorientingly wild and unkempt. She was no longer my feisty, bitchy, exacting, loving, confidante.

At twenty-two, I was in the thrall of my new life in NYC and I lacked the grace and courage required to see her regularly. I could not recognise her in the wrecked, bed-bound husk she had become. To my shame, I called occasionally and visited rarely.

When Nana died, we held only a graveside service. The double plot was near her sister Irene's, overlooking the Bradlees / Stop and Shop – a discount department store *and* a convenience store and a favourite haunt of both sisters.

At the time of her mother's death, Mom was practical. It

was only many years later that I could see her regret. Ruth had offered her children to Nana in lieu of a relationship with her herself. Ruth had shouldered responsibility for her parents long before, but in the moment that she was released from that burden, she had to take up the mantle of 'next up to die.' A heavy robe passed down from matriarch to daughter.

It was Uncle Lew who was the most undone by Nana's death. 'It's your mother,' he said, throwing up his hands. As we sat over a bottle of wine the night before her funeral, he repeated, 'you only have one mother.' This, despite the many years of thrice weekly Freudian analysis sessions because the mother who adored him also ignored his coming out and denied his queerness, foisting unwanted dates along with her wedding ring on him. Any pride she took in his achievements was heavily overshadowed by his failure to marry.

On his way through to his parental visits, Lew would stop in White Plains to collect me. No awkward questions would be asked in my presence, no pleas for marriage; I was the buffer zone that facilitated their *entente cordiale*. Years later, he presented me with that heavy, gold ring of overlapping oak leaves to use as my wedding ring.

After the funeral, we packed up the condo. Clearing closets and distributing mementos, most of the contents going to furnish my brother's first family home. We also packed up Papa and settled him into a nursing home in a Federalist building on the green in Salem, Massachusetts, site of the famous witch trials. Increasingly cranky and withdrawn, he faded away and died less than a year later.

I waited for Dad to call back in torturous anticipation, fear prickling along my skin like a rash. I tried to embed my mother in my belly, where Dexter used to be, safe and whole. I poured myself into tending to him. If I cradled Dexter with the utmost tenderness, it was her coddled and embraced; if I

pressed my cheek to his and brushed against the silken plump-
ness, it was her caressed; if I blew hot breath into his back,
rubbing to spread its heat, it was her warmed and cosseted.

I prepared dinner with the same reverent prayerfulness,
mindfulness slowed to a glacial pace. I sliced garlic in precise
translucent wafers, I sectioned tomatoes into exact quarters.
This perfection would keep her whole. I would not step on a
single crack; I would not break my mother's back.

'She made it through surgery but they're talking about
collateral damage,' my father finally reported. I sat on the
bed, rocking mutely from side to side as if I were holding
the baby, but he was safe in Simon's arms. My father's voice
was stretched and scared and I could picture him, sitting on
her side of their bed, his palm against his upturned forehead,
his eyes squinting.

'What do you mean collateral damage?' I finally asked.

'Brain damage,' he says.

Again, I heard the hissing and snap of electricity in my
head. She is her brain. I want to hold it, bathe it, lick it clean.

'I think you should come down,' my father tells me. I
refused to hear what he hasn't said. 'You better hurry.'

'She's two-dimensional, flat, like she was run over by a
truck,' my father warned us, slapping his outstretched hands
together, his eyes screwed up tight and his mouth gaping
open like a bass on ice. He looked like a cartoon drawing of
someone who's ingested poison, with x's for eyes and a lolling
tongue. He's trying his best to prepare us.

Before our arrival he alone has been immersed in the
details and reports and tests but now that we're there, he
spews out the story, words tumbling out of him. How she
simply bent down to pick up a carton of milk that had fallen
out of the fridge. How the night before it happened she had
spent hours in the garden tending to Irmgard's god-damned

heirloom tomatoes. How, Birdie, the housekeeper had been working in the house and was there; how she had kept right on vacuuming even after the ambulance arrived.

'If I hadn't been there; she would just have gone and laid down and she would have died.'

How the ambulance was so quick to get there; how he followed in his car. These words conjure an inappropriate image in my mind of Mr. Bean following an ambulance so closely that it looks like they're towing him, so close that they can't open the back doors while he blithely steps out of his car and strides into the hospital.

'She knows what happened, she was conscious when I told the doctor that her mother died the same way.'

Lew turned bilious at this. I feel a punch of dread recalling Lew's same warning about Nana. 'You won't recognise her.'

Dad was not wrong. She was a mass of tubes and wounds and pain. She sometimes rose to consciousness like a fish surfacing for air. Her liver-flecked, work-worn hands wafted and weaved in familiar gestures; they alone did her talking, performing solo, where they were once part of a whole ensemble. Her shrugs, nods and eyebrows acting in concert to broadcast her pain and discomfort, her fear and confusion, the countless alarmed questions she couldn't enunciate.

My father declined a proposed CAT scan. 'Why? If she's brain dead, what difference does it make and if she's not, it'll be uncomfortable and upsetting. Why? Just so they can charge for more tests?' he railed.

Only two of us were allowed in at a time. Sometimes she was senseless, a mute slab puffed and deflated by tubes and beeps in the vast, cold room. I stood by her head, combing her hair while my brother tried to reach her through his violin; the notes saying 'Are you listening, Mom? Now come back!' I crooned songs from the *Oh Brother Where Art Thou* soundtrack, which were the lullabies I sang to Dexter. The songs seemed both prayerful and hopeful, throat-aching songs that are more like begging than singing. There was still dried blood in her hair, at the base of her neck. I was her simian daughter, picking at her big grey head.

Temporarily awake again, her eyes widened in exaggerated shock and mock horror when my father announced that he had bought a cell phone. Her shock that he had bought such a thing – and without consulting her – turned to terror because the situation she was in required one.

We sprawled around a large table in a corner of the hospital cafe that we had commandeered as our command post. Leah and I took turns seeing Mom and looking after Dexter, swinging him to each other, still in his sling, like a satchel. Uncle Lew, who has been almost a third parent throughout our lives, appeared crumpled and reduced in the face of his older sister's crisis. He'd become one of us, all lost siblings together.

He was just back from another trip to Brazil where he went to bask in the sunshine and revel in the beautiful men. In the last few years, since he'd had an undetected heart attack followed by bypass surgery, he had shed a load of excess weight and some of his inhibitions and self-imposed constraints. He seemed to accrue successive boyfriends on each trip without relinquishing any of the previous ones. 'My dance card just gets fuller,' he shrugged with a mixture of pride and faux modesty.

When I offered him the sack of goji berries picked at random from the health food store, he scoffed, batting them away in dismissal. 'You sure I can't tempt you?'

'I don't believe in that nonsense,' he started as I read out the benefits.

' …supports your immune system, source of vitamin C,

good for your eyesight, prevents liver damage, promotes weight loss, improves virility, boosts testosterone ...'

'Oh, I'll give them a try. They can't hurt, right?'

'Gobble, gobble,' my sister and I jinxed together, parodying Lew's phrase repeated at each Thanksgiving as he bears the loaded plate of turkey to the table.

We erupt in laughter, a continuance of the banter that is the baseline of all our family gatherings regardless of the occasion.

When we weren't with Mom, we stuck together. We felt a certain safety in numbers that defied logic but amounted to the closing of our slim ranks against the invading forces of collateral damage and death. We slept where we could in my parents' cottage. On reflex, I shoved Dexter onto my breast when he woke hungry and crying in the night, more to silence him than comfort him, lest we wake any of the slumbering bodies around us.

I had just started to get the hang of things with Dexter and now this. Little did I know that this was the first in long line of 'now this's to come in the early years of his life.

Only family was allowed but we offered to take Irmgard to visit a sometimes conscious Ruth. In the hospital room, she sat down formally and crossed her hands, 'Hello, Ruth.' I handed Mom a clipboard that Leah thought to bring so that my mother could write what the tubes prevented her from saying.

She peered at Irmgard and then wrote, 'How are _you_?' underlining the 'you'. Then she wrote 'pain', and we got the nurse. Ruth remembered none of this.

Dad couldn't bring himself to articulate what had happened. 'When Ruth had the incident, the ...' and he grabbed a word from the headlines, 'tsunami ...'

'The mommy tsunami,' I finished for him.

Back at the house, I discovered Ruth's threadbare t-shirt in the laundry basket, torn down the front by the medics to get to her chest.

'Did you tell Paddington?' I asked my father. Paddington had taken up vigilant residence on my mother's side of the bed.

'He was here; he saw the whole damn thing.'

On her bedside table, propped against a red Mr Peanut cup chock-full of pens and pencils – another relic from my childhood – is a letter I wrote to my mother in the first weeks of Dexter's life. I felt compelled to write to her, I explained, because I had failed in my first task as a mother; I had not given birth to Dexter. And because I hadn't, I felt I had some lesser claim to motherhood than other women who succeeded in giving birth naturally. This will be my last regret, I boldly declared. HA! I had barely dipped a toe in the bottomless pit of parental regret.

It hadn't yet occurred to me that my separation from Dexter and the passivity with which I had given birth, served to mirror Ruth's experience. Like hers, my baby came to me via the hands of others. And like her, there was a gulf of separation from my baby to overcome. Are you my mirror?

Neither did it occur to me that my experience mirrored my birth mother's but, for her, the separation from her baby was without end.

From the moment I was told that I didn't have enough amniotic fluid, I felt wrong-footed. I don't know why I excoriated myself in the way that I did, why I felt so self-scathingly unqualified for motherhood. I only know that it took a long time to find my feet.

My letter was a declaration of final regret; written in earnest and utterly futile. It was propped there, as a prompt to Mom to write back when she'd thought about what she wanted to say. I hope she would have told me to snap out of it. You were brainwashed, you're a mom no matter how your baby gets to you! A C-section is not a crime! It would have been short and thoughtful and meant the world to me, but she never wrote it.

9

FRESH SHORES (2005-2007)

'Go live your life,' my father urged as we left Mom's room at the rehabilitation hospital. She had been lying in her own filth when we arrived that morning. Appalled, we spent the rest of the morning trying to get someone to clean her up. She pulled at the wires linking her to the surrounding machines, and tried to make a break for the door. 'She's a puller,' one of the nurses said to us in an accusatory tone, as if we, or indeed my unconscious mother, had some say in the matter. There wasn't a damn thing I could do about any of it.

How the hell was I supposed to 'go live my life' when half my heart beat inside of Dexter and the other half was on life support in North Carolina? How could I leave the country and my unconscious mother and move to London? My mother's compromised and precarious state had zapped my enthusiasm for the looming move. It was with a deadened heart and leaden steps that I dragged myself away from her side.

The news of bombings in London on the morning of July 7, accompanied by images of a horrifically mangled double-decker bus, a mere ten days before we were due to fly, only added to my overwhelming feeling of dread.

The night before the movers were due, my frenetic rushing from one room to another was stopped only by my locking myself into the bathroom until I'd packed everything in it. Simon alternately packed important papers or burnt redundant ones in the fireplace. We had not started packing the kitchen when the movers arrived at 6 a.m. the next morning. By the time we tossed the smouldering fire grate into the back of the van, I never wanted to see any of it again.

We arrived at Heathrow on the morning of Tuesday, July 19th with fourteen pieces of luggage including the living room blinds that we had neglected to take down until the last minute; our poor cat had flown steerage. We embarked on an apartment search in West London, near Simon's brother, on Thursday because whether or not I ever wanted to the see the 20-foot container full of our belongings again, it was on its way to London and we needed somewhere to put it and the cat before Simon started work on the following Monday.

Over the screaming sirens on the Shepherds Bush Road, I overheard a teenaged boy say in passing, 'I was really nervous about the first bombings, but I'm quite relaxed about these.' I took a less sanguine approach to that day's attempted bombings and was further unsettled when Jean Charles de Menezes, mistaken for one of the would-be bombers, was shot dead in Stockwell tube station the next day.

In New York, I had been bewildered by a lack of sleep and the never-ending job that is new motherhood. It was the first job that I couldn't quit and walk away from. I swayed and bobbed in the living room in the early hours of the morning as revellers drifted by after last call as I had done not long ago. Both Dexter and I howled in lonely frustration as I tore at my hair in the first bath I had taken in seven days while he made his bouncy chair nearly flip with the power of his vigorously kicking legs. I cannot fathom why I ever thought I would be good at this. Nothing came easily or naturally, not even breast feeding. So I swallowed my nausea at the retch-inducing name and attended my appointment with a lactation consultant at Femsurge. I learned the extremely useful 'football' hold to help Dexter's powerful jaw relieve my aching breasts of milk and dutifully crunched the prescribed garlic to cure my infected nipples. But I still lacked enough supply, so I supplemented Dexter's diet with formula. Each unnatural intervention was another blow to my confidence and a further black mark against my parenting credentials. But no matter how dispirited I was, at least in New York the rest of my life was recognisable. Sort of. At least I knew how to make an appointment for a lactation consultant at a place called Femsurge. Soon, that would seem like a dream, a good dream even.

We found a suitable apartment in Chiswick on the Saturday morning, two days before Simon started work. It was in our price range and nicer by far than anything else we'd seen. 'We'll take it,' I said. The apartment was unoccupied and in need of no repairs, but it wouldn't be ready for a few weeks. This was apparently normal procedure and as the boat with our container was still on the water, I decamped to my sister-in-law's flat in Bournemouth with Dexter. Not knowing what else to do, I paraded the pram up and down the board-walk for miles. Occasionally, someone would coo at the baby but mostly my interactions involved someone handing me a shucked sock of Dexter's with a look of disappointment.

'I don't know what I'm doing here,' I told Simon, 'I don't understand my life.' Naturally, he was defensive. Technically, I was a trailing spouse, but that term usually applies to people who have been offered a brilliant opportunity and so much money they can't refuse. We, on the other hand, had moved to London as a destination and it was a rational, mutual decision, despite being cash poor. It seemed like the opportune time as both our jobs had ended and Dexter was just six months old. Besides, I had always wanted to live in Europe, and as one friend said, 'the best thing about London is Paris.' But in the wake of my mother's illness and my unexpected post-partum self-doubt and isolation, I feel like I have been dragged to London by my hair.

Speaking English fooled me into a false sense of fluency. As our move date approached, Simon started giving me 'British' lessons. I couldn't figure out if he was just anxious on my behalf or if people would dislike me for saying 'diaper' instead of 'nappy'. I sneered at Simon's concerns about me fitting in, but I started seeing his point.

My sense of alienation was fuelled by not knowing how anything functioned. In New York I could yell, wheedle, chivvy and cajole to get what I wanted. Here, I didn't understand how things worked, I only knew how I expected them to work but they didn't. I mostly encountered unfailingly polite people, but *polite* is very different from *useful*. To the question at the post office, 'can I send this overnight?' the polite response was 'no, I'm sorry madam, that is not a service we provide,' which while undeniably correct was also entirely useless. No other service was offered. In New York, I would expect a withering look to accompany, 'no, lady, but if you want it there in two days, it's five dollars.'

I was also slow to understand or navigate the British reserve and sense of embarrassment. Brits, otherwise parsimonious to the point of stingy when showing emotion, are positively lavish when it comes to embarrassment, so that even if I weren't embarrassed, they would jump right in and be embarrassed on my behalf. Rather than an embarrassment of riches, it's a richness of embarrassment. I would not be adopting this mannerism. I had spent years brazening it out while my mother picked through the trash in our local park for the 5 cent deposit bottles or pocketed the free rolls at restaurants; I was vulcanized to withstand embarrassment. Long gone were the days when I would blush to a fluorescent pink at the slightest provocation.

Sometimes I couldn't figure out if I came off as obnoxious and demanding, living up to a New York stereotype even when I was trying to be reasonable, or if the other person was just being an asshole. Maybe I was prickly and paranoid, very possible, or then again, maybe it was assumed I was a ball-busting bitch because I was from New York. It was hard to tell.

I found a mushroom growing out of the back of the toilet. A big mushroom, the size of my out-stretched hand. It was white and as translucent as the porcelain it bloomed from. I'm not a professional plumber but I figured a mushroom growing out of the back of the toilet meant there was a problem with the toilet. The estate agent who managed the one-bedroom flat took some convincing that a mushroom was an emergency but at my insistence sent a plumber several days later. 'Seriously, is it normal to have mushrooms the size of my hand in the restrooms here?' I quizzed Simon.

'It's loo or toilet, and no.'

In the meantime, I felt that there was water seeping up in the hallway outside the toilet. I say 'felt', because although I couldn't see any water, there was a squidgy feeling underfoot so I jumped up and down on it for a while and then put a tea towel down which came away wet. In my, still unprofessional opinion, I assumed this water was related to the mushroom growing out of the back of the toilet.

When the plumber arrived, he tinkered about in the loo

117

for a bit, drank two cups of tea, looked sour that I didn't have biscuits or instant coffee and then declared that he had fixed the problem and went on his jolly old way.

Several days went by and the hallway outside the bathroom still felt squidgy. I bounced around some more and brandished the sopping towel as evidence at Simon, dramatically wringing it out in the sink in front of him. I called the estate agent again. 'No there is not another mushroom but it's still leaking!' I went the extra mile and laid in biscuits and instant coffee for the plumber's return.

'What happened?' he asked as soon as he was in the door.

'Nothing *happened*, it's just still leaking.' I bounced a little to prove my point.

'But you said it was the toilet, I fixed the toilet,' he accused.

'Well, I'm not a plumber. There was a mushroom coming out of the back of the toilet, so I thought it was the toilet.'

'You called the agency again so they think I didn't fix it,' he was visibly angry.

'Well, there's water on the floor so you might have fixed the toilet but there's still a leak.' Not so easily mollified, he ostentatiously refused the biscuits and coffee.

An hour later, he cheerfully called me over. He'd pulled up all the floorboards in the hallway, the only point of access to the kitchen and loo, to expose a pipe spraying water like a garden sprinkler. Also revealed was London, in all its dirty glory just below my feet. Earwigs scattered like a fleeing army, centipedes and beetles scrambled from the light.

'You were right, love. Look at that. It'll take a couple of days to fix that lot, maybe a week.'

I am both astonished and alarmed by the amount of nature that surrounds us in London. In New York, animal life beyond the domesticated generally compromised of rats, pigeons, cockroaches, water bugs, squirrels, sparrows and ants. During a summer thunderstorm in Brooklyn, I was drawn to the window by a deep lowing, a sound from my childhood. A bullfrog squatted, sheltering under a broad leaf, belching his heart out. The wildest creature in all Brooklyn, where had he come from?

Beleaguered though I was, I couldn't battle on all fronts, so I funnelled all my anxieties into the encroach of wildlife into our flat; after the mushroom, came the snails. When my dearest friend moved to Prague, she entrusted her cat to us on the basis that there were no screen windows or doors in Prague and the declawed cat would be defenceless against predators. We had gone through great expense and bother to import said cat, now named Monkeypox or The Pox or Poxy or (rarely) MKPX, to London. The lack of screened windows or doors didn't faze the cat but posed other problems.

'There were some snails on the windowsill in the kitchen, did you see where they went?' I asked Simon as we got into bed on a rainy night.

'They were heading for the fruit bowl,' he answered sleepily.

'Did you shut the window?'

'No, it's raining, this is the time of year when they head inside.'

'Really? How fine a mesh would it take to keep snails out?' but exhaustion wins out over outrage.

The next morning, the nectarines had been nibbled, the navigational trails of the hungry snails evident in munched skin.

Our upstairs neighbours, Sarah and her daughter, had been away when we first moved in but returned some weeks later. From behind the blinds of our front room, I peered at the woman as she stood, hands on hips, assessing the state of her front garden. She had wiry, curly hair like me and was

119

refreshingly unreserved, earthy and forthright. She was kind enough to take us under her generous wing and helped initiate me in the ways of my new world.

When I started awake to what sounded like an infant being stabbed to death, I was grateful Sarah had warned me of the fox slinking through the back garden, its rasp desolate and desperate in the night.

Adding to the ambient anxiety in which I lived and moved, news of my mother's condition and progress was sporadic. Communication was via email or pre-paid international phone cards to cut the expense. My father was too busy tending to my mother's needs and my uncle and brother assumed that my sister was updating me. My sister and I both had our arms full to bursting with our families, but we also weren't speaking to one another after a bitter argument, each of us equally entrenched in our vantage point and incensed at the outrageous insensitivity and obtuseness of the other.

Shortly after I headed to London, Leah had uprooted her family, moving them from Westchester to Chapel Hill to help coax Mom back to health. She was head cheerleader, coach and advocate and after almost four months in the hospital Mom was eventually released back to the health centre on campus. I finally hear my mother's voice on the phone for the first time in over five months. She is too breathless to say more than, 'When are you coming?'

I decided to wean Dexter at nine months so I could go see my mother. My new pattern seemed to be to flounder until I found a rhythm that worked and then have it ripped to smithereens by circumstance or tear it up myself. I buried my nose in his yeasty neck and clutched his bed-warm pudge in his fuzzy, duckling pyjamas. He was still smiling when I handed him to Simon and turned away feeling like a traitor.

I carried with me the guilt of leaving Dexter but at least the extra tonne of Jewish daughter guilt was lightened by a week of fitting into the intricate patterns of care woven around my mother by my sister and father. Without their determined devotion, she would never have had the will to dig deep enough to recover. Weakened and dependent though she was, my mother was back. She wanted all the details of life in London and Dexter. We could actually hug and when I left her, unlike the last time, she knew where I was going. At the very least, your mother should know which country you live in. But the plaintive final phrase remained, 'When are you coming back?'

Life back in London was lighter with lines of communication now restored with my mother and sister. Frequent-flyer Uncle Lew was our first visitor. 'She is happy, she is resilient,' he reported back to the family and returned two months later en route to Paris for Christmas, which he never spent at home in Washington DC. Dexter and I joined him for a lunch of roast duck in prunes on the Seine. It was true, an excellent and delicious thing about London was Paris. We found a rhythm, and friends to meet at the swings and playdates in the park, and Dexter crawled then walked and talked. We flew to join joyful family reunions on the North Carolina shore.

I called off my war against wildlife. I resisted petting an adorable, spiny hedgehog on my way home one evening. Parakeets swooped through the gloaming in Chiswick House Park, bickering in packs. Each day for a month, Dexter and I visited a ladybird larva and clocked its progress to pupa and eventually into a ladybird. We watched coots build their nests under the schoolmasterly eye of the ever-present heron and counted the terrapins that basked on a tree trunk protruding from the pond. Sarah took us to the kitchen gardens and while she watered, we looped and larked through the beds in the golden hour. On a magnificent afternoon, the edifice of

Chiswick House was made red by an infestation of ladybirds, an auspicious omen I thought.

And just as my cup threatened to runneth over, it cracked.

I found out later that I was the last to know that Uncle Lew had lung cancer. What made me sadder, was finding out that when he did call me to let me know the terrible news at the end of September 2007, he hid the truth of what he knew, telling me he had 18–24 months, not the 6–12 he told everyone else. He would end up lying to me on the last day of his life, just as he had on that phone call.

His cancer was inoperable and so he would undergo a course of chemotherapy, 'not the most aggressive so it shouldn't be too bad,' he said. Leah was speaking to him on a Saturday morning in early November when he suffered a stroke.

Dexter and I had been scheduled to visit for Thanksgiving and flew to Washington where Lew's friend Maureen picked us up and drove us directly to the rehab hospital. Lew had mentioned her to me only once, in the context of a trip to Ireland. Even Lew's oldest friend Richard hadn't heard of her. 'Who's this Maureen person?' he asked me. This Maureen person turned out to be an astonishingly kind and caring friend who Lew had originally met through his real estate consultancy work. All the compartments of his life that he worked so hard to keep separate from each other would be laid bare in the face of illness and death.

Lew smiles and waves his familiar regal wave but then rolls his eyes and says, 'I hate this hotel.' Maureen and I smile over this verbal switch. 'One more day, you're coming home tomorrow.'

When we got to the rehab hospital the next morning, I had to whip Dexter out of Maureen's car just as he started to vomit; it landed mostly in a puddle on the pavement. Disaster

Reunion Marks Start of Scene 2 of Unusual Drama

Miriam Lindenmaier, in photo at left, on the way to being arraigned on a charge that she had participated in a plot to defraud two insurance companies by pretending to have drowned in a boating mishap in July. Riding to the arraignment in another car are two others charged in the alleged plot, Alvin Brodie, at right, and Thomas Martin.

The New York Times (by Patrick A. Burns)

Dr. and Mrs. Werner A. Lindenmaier after being reunited with their daughter in Bronx yesterday. Until this reunion, the parents had not known that their daughter was alive

Alvin on the steps of the Bronx County Court on his way to being arraigned

Ruth at her engagement party

Ruth and Sy

Donna with Grandparents Lily and Aaron in North Miami Beach

Donna with her parents and Paul on their 50th anniversary 2006

Tony and Donna, Florida January 2020

Mira

Ruth with Dexter 2005

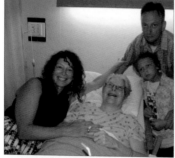

Donna, Mira,
Simon & Dexter

Donna, Dexter and Simon

averted, we proceeded to Operation Liberate Lew. I reviewed the thick binder of information with the discharge nurse and signed the release forms. We collected the bags of prescriptions and then Lew progressed, stately and slow, out of the hospital. Lew, though hunched and weak, was purposeful. So determined to reach the car that he was impervious when we tried to steer him around the malevolent pile of puke. He carried on, stepped squarely in it and settled himself in the front seat, looking satisfied with his efforts and grateful to be in familiar and luxurious surroundings; he had the exact same model Lexus.

We managed to have a normal enough Thanksgiving with Leah and her children and Oliver, Lew's dog. Oliver was a gorgeous and exuberant yellow lab, abused as a puppy and then rescued. Indulged and ecstatic in my uncle's company, he feared men and other dogs. Lew had been deeply ashamed when he was kicked out of doggy day care for biting another dog's ear. Oliver mostly communed with Lew, asleep either on the sofa in the den or his bed upstairs. The stroke butchered Lew's speech and muddled his thoughts but enough was intelligible that he seemed almost himself.

Leah did the turkey and the 'gobble, gobble' honours which earned a smile from Lew. We left the house only to go to the park and walk the dog. We couldn't leave Lew unattended, but I also couldn't walk Oliver and push Dexter's buggy at the same time. For the most part, Oliver ignored other dogs but if they barked at him, he was all fight and flight – lunging at their throats with only my pathetic upper arm strength holding him back.

I changed our tickets for the first time and postponed our trip to see Mom and Dad. Leah and the kids left for home and Dexter and I stayed with Lew and Oliver.

I attempted to keep my three charges on separate floors of

the house. I had just started potty training Dexter the month before and I should have abandoned it but since I'd started, I stupidly persisted under the duress of this latest catastrophe. When the dog wasn't with Lew he had a penchant for socks and dirty pull-up pants and Dexter didn't close doors. I hustled up and down the stairs to Lew up top, Oliver, barking on the sofa at passing trade and Dexter amusing himself by bumping his butt up and down the carpeted stairs to the basement.

Lew wanted my help in getting his affairs in order and handed over paperwork and bills to sort through. I wrote cheques for him to sign. He'd never had a signature so much as a scrawl of incomprehensible letters that changed over the years; the stroke made it no worse. He was ashamed about the lung cancer diagnosis, to have been dumb enough to chain-smoke Chesterfields for forty years, and he was now embarrassed by the stroke damage. Beyond immediate family, he would speak only to his lawyer and one or two very close friends.

Chemo treatment was suspended after the stoke (which was induced by the aggressive chemo), but weeks later it was back on the schedule. Maureen agreed to take us to the first appointment. While Lew underwent chemo, I had promised Dexter a trip to the zoo.

When Dex and I got up at six the next morning, we found Lew in a foul mood. Anxious about the chemo, he'd been awake and dressed, with a terrible headache since 5 a.m. Lew eschewed my help. To make tea, he placed a teabag in cold water in a mug and then put the mug into the microwave. When I cited this as evidence of the stroke damage, to my shock, Leah assured me that some people actually made tea that way!

'Maureen is picking us up in a few minutes,' he snapped at

me just before seven, 'and you're not even dressed.'

'Oh no, honey, she's not coming until nine, your appointment is at 9:30.'

He was momentarily shaken but came back fighting. 'You have a whole day's work to do, you can't possibly go to the zoo!'

'Sure we can, I'll get it all done, it's not that much.' I kept my voice even, but I was close to tears. The zoo was the only thing I had promised Dexter that week. I couldn't and wouldn't take it away from him.

The doctor, taking in the baby and the buggy, greeted us peremptorily, wanting to get the chemo under way until I held up the page of questions compiled by me in consultation with the family. So, he stashed us in a consulting room where Lew laid back on the examining table, his legs dangling over the edge as if he were on a dock with his feet dabbling in the water below. Further up, his arms were crossed over his chest as if in final rest.

'How are you feeling?' the doctor boomed as the door flew open. Lew lurched up and shook his head. I enquired about his medications and asked for a review.

'What kind of stroke did he suffer? Blood clot or bleed?'

'Blood clot, sometimes chemo throws up clots.' He shrugged in a 'go figure?' kind of way.

Once I had checked off all my questions, we settled Lew into the BarcaLounger-style reclining chair with his chemo drip and jumped in a cab.

Dexter and I ran through the zoo, dizzy in the sunlight. We played peek-a-boo with Tai Shan, the baby panda who was mugging for the camera and stared back at the massive owls. We cranked a penny through the coin press to make an oblong lion coin and bought Mom a panda, a miniature version of my Holly bought here in the '70s. We grabbed a quick lunch across the street. Our faces were still split in smiles when we burst through the doors to see Lew sitting in the waiting room, slumped and ashen. My stomach churned with guilt and flooded my mouth with nausea.

He said nothing until we got home and then only wanted the dog. They retired to bed for the rest of the day. He came down for dinner but rejected the risotto I made in favour of grilled cheese sandwiches. As he put them together, his loveless, cooking shortcuts reminded me that he has lived his whole life alone except for a few years with a boyfriend.

I was trying to keep Dexter out of the kitchen but he was hell-bent on grabbing Oliver's tail who, in his turn, was hell-bent on sharing Lew's sandwiches. I scooped up Dexter and deposited him in the dining room. By the time I retuned to the kitchen, Oliver had gulped down one of the sandwiches.

Lew sat down, defeated, with the single sandwich. 'I know I might not be the perfect person to be here right now, but I really want to be here with you.' He nodded silently and went back up to bed.

I put Dexter to bed and walked Oliver; I brought Lew his medication and some tea. I opened some wine and called Mom to report the day's events. I was on horribly familiar ground, consumed with worry about two generations at once. I reeled with the responsibility that seemed to have been handed down to us children when we weren't looking. These are the things that my parents used to shield us from. 'I'm sorry you're coming second again,' I whispered to Dexter when I got into bed.

With the same blunt obstinacy which kept me soldiering on with the potty training, I forged ahead with a plan to visit my parents for a night against both my better judgement and my sister's advice. I hoped it was enough to install a medical alarm system and arrange for Maureen to visit in the evening, but no sooner had she left than another fucking clot shot to Lew's brain and caused a stroke.

The next day, back at 'the same damn hotel,' I propped Dexter on my hip so I could sign consent forms for vena cava filters to be fitted in Lew's legs; he lay next to us on the operating table practising the corpse pose.

It didn't fully register when the nurse said that Lew had 'mild pneumonia', I was too busy announcing Dexter's first poo in the toilet. The nurses, the only witnesses, dutifully clapped for a shyly smiling Dexter.

It had been almost a month since we had arrived and everyone agreed that it was time we went home now that Lew was stable. I was planning to come back to stay for the month of January.

'We're going home for real this time,' I told a weary Dexter. I had said goodbye to Lew the night before and was writing up some handover notes for my brother, who was taking my place the following week.

'What's happening?' my mother asked on the phone. 'The hospital called and said they wanted to intubate Lew and he refused.'

I called the hospital but his nurse told me that was not the case, 'no, he's just had some treatment to clear his lungs but he's fine.'

Dexter was gleeful in the taxi, singing 'On the road again' at top note. Leah called while we were in the queue, 'I think Lew is worse, are you sure you should go?'

'I have to go,' I wailed, 'I'm at the airport.'

We had checked in and were on the airport bus headed to the gate. This time it was Simon on the phone. He had spoken with Leah. 'If you want to say goodbye to Lew, I'm afraid that you need to go back. You won't have another chance.'

I am completely baffled by this turn of events. 'But the

nurse told me he was fine!' I called the hospital again from a fax machine at the gate. In Lew's room, his friend Jim picked up, 'Where are you calling from?' mystified because he knew I was supposed to be on a plane.

'The airport, is he dying?'

'Yes,' he said, 'he doesn't want to live any more. He's sleeping now. It took me a long time to figure out what he wanted but he asked me for the suicide drugs that Dr. Kavorkian uses.'

'Why didn't they tell me?'

'He didn't want you to know, he said you're too emotional.'

I never thought of being emotional as a negative, but in their final moments who wants the terror and pathos of impending death mirrored back to them, no matter how empathetically? A particular horror perhaps for Lew, who kept us all in our compartments, whose heart, like an old-fashioned hardware store nail cabinet, had many more than just four chambers.

'It's not good,' Lew said when I got to the hospital.

'I know.' I told him I loved him and that his sister would be there tomorrow. I stayed until he slept and I did not cry. He remained unconscious from then on and died after Mom and Dad and Leah visited the following day. He was sixty-seven.

A few days after Dexter and I finally returned home, completely out of nowhere, our friend Warren, who was younger than Lew, died suddenly in Connecticut. Younger still, our upstairs neighbour Sarah had also unravelled in our absence, her mental health coming undone as if pulled loose by a thread. She had lost her footing and her faith in herself and the possibility of a healthy future. By spring she too had passed away. In mute protest, Dexter gave death the silent treatment and stopped speaking for a month.

It had been a bruising season full of hail and struggle. In the aftermath of the deaths, we moved house, further unsettling Dexter. I took my sister's advice and packed every single item of Dexter's. When we got to the new flat, he cried 'I want to go home,' over and over again for forty-five minutes until it sunk in what I was showing him. I picked up item after item, torn pages out of books, halved plastic action figures, random bits of Mr Potato Head parts, toy car wheels, puzzle pieces. We brought it all. He sat on my lap and stared in wonder at all his worldly possessions arrayed before him.

10

THE MIRROR CRACKS FROM SIDE TO SIDE(2009)

Lew stated clearly in his will that he did not wish to have a funeral of any kind and instead wanted us to travel to Paris as a family and spread his ashes in the Seine. To that end, I asked the crematorium to Fedex his ashes to me in London. The best thing about London is its proximity to the Seine. It turned out to be a bit of a dog leg for the ashes, but it seemed like a good idea at the time.

We had only held an informal gathering at Lew's house soon after he died in December 2007 but as it was just before Christmas, not many could attend. He did not expressly forbid a memorial so we planned a celebration of his life with his many friends and associates to be held in Washington DC in May 2008, after which we would depart, with Lew's ashes in tow, for Paris so the ashes could have saved themselves a trip and stayed state-side after all.

Ashes do not travel well. Because of their density, they show up on x-ray scanners as a dangerous, black object that must be further investigated. This is the case whether your cremains are in your checked bags or hand luggage, which poses a more personal dilemma. Are you comfortable carrying the surprisingly heavy cremains of your loved one in your handbag or are you okay with putting them amongst your clothes to be manhandled and crushed with all the other baggage? There are no good choices with ashes, there are no winners.

For the flight to Washington, I went with cremains in the checked bag, as my hand-baggage allowance was taken up by Dexter's paraphernalia. It seemed even more blasphemous to tuck Lew's ashes in Dexter's blanky than wrapping a spring coat around him and wedging him between the shoes.

After the memorial, Simon, Dexter and I had a stop-over en route to Paris so I decided to put Lew in our hand luggage for that leg of the journey. We had a short time in Paris and what if our luggage got lost and we didn't get Lew back in time to put him in the Seine as a family? Of course, I only remembered to do this at the airport.

'Shit, I need to get Lew,' I exclaimed to Simon. We didn't remember which bag he was in and so had to unzip and unpack both big bags, muttering to ourselves suspiciously, almost certainly flagging a bag search.

Simon and I were boisterous and rebellious going through security, which, along with travelling with cremains, is never a good idea. We were relegated, as a family, to the glass box as the security guards pawed through our bags, bristling with self-importance. It also didn't help that, when they held up Lew and asked, 'what's this?', I burst out laughing, 'It's my uncle!'

As per the instructions in his will, we had booked rooms in Lew's favourite hotel, the Hotel d'Albe on rue de la Harpe next to the Place Saint-Michel. After dinner, on the Saturday night, Leah, Paul and I left Lew's friend David's apartment and headed down the Rue Mazarine to the Seine carrying Lew's ashes, a feather boa and a collection of Mardi Gras beads that had been a fixture in his living room. We had a vague idea of wearing the beads and saying some words, but a sudden thunderstorm pummelled us just as we got to the river. With the nine p.m. chimes ringing out from Notre Dame, we recklessly tossed the whole lot into the Seine. Some of Lew's ashes coated my wet, sandalled feet. Back at the Hotel d'Albe, I sat on the side of the tub and carefully rinsed them off, Lew's ashes swirling away through the plumbing of his spiritual home.

A year later, when each passing day felt less like a battle for survival, Simon and I planned an actual holiday to Corfu. The week before we went, my world tilted with another 'now this'. Leah called with the shattering news that Mom had been diagnosed with lymphoma and had three months to live. She ended up eking it out to seven.

At first, Mom and Dad didn't want visitors, fearing infection while she underwent chemo, but I soon joined the ranks of the international commuters, leaving London on a Thursday or Friday and returning from my parents on Sunday or Monday, once with only two weeks in between. I knew the menu and the flight crew and I recognised my regular fellow passengers on what I dubbed the 'GlaxoSmithKlein Express', the daily American Airlines round-trip flight between Heathrow and North Carolina's Raleigh–Durham research triangle. Simon shouldered the childcare when I was away, which provided a partial distraction from his father's own diagnosis of myeloma and the grim prognosis which accompanied it. When we had last seen him, he was puffy from chemo but still in good spirits.

In the final week of August 2009, we amassed at Mom and

Dad's house before heading out to the beach for our family reunion without them. We tried to convince them that she could go to the hospital in nearby Morehead City if required, but Mom was not for budging. From that point on, travel off campus would be restricted to medical appointments.

Painful tumours had sprung up on her head. The pain patches she applied stuck up on her head, making it look like she was getting her hair highlighted. Leah and I carefully shaved the hair around the tumours, so we could apply the patches directly. She was small and sunken but cheered by our ministrations. 'How do I look?' she asked with her impish smile.

Mom worked diligently on what she and Dad called her Doomsday Manual, listing all the payments she made, who gets what amount for their birthdays, how often the sheets on the bed needed changing and when to launder the bathmat among other matters of importance. She also sent me further musings on her life. An email from July 14, 2009 read: 'Probably today (Tues) you will get an email with a few more pages. I think this may be everything I have saved. If I do [write more], are there any topics you would like?'

Two days later, there was a one-line email: 'Another day about the same pain level.'

We sat on the bed and went through a pile of her writings. Some old essays, some attempts at fiction, scraps of ideas and thoughts; I had a similar pile of scribblings and snippets at home. One in particular, a half page of scrawled short story idea appealed to us both. It concerned a girl in her early teens who has a menacing experience on the beach at Marshfield, a sort of coming-of-age story. Nana and Papa had once had a house in Marshfield, a seaside town south of Boston.

'Can I do something with this?' I asked.

'Sure, I thought it was a pretty good idea.'

For the next few months, I worked on the story, *Marshfield*, with her. I sent her the pages as I progressed. It allowed us to focus on something other than her death. It gave us a break from my nearly nightly calls to ask her any and every question I could think of. But eventually, I awkwardly and prematurely ended the story; it had become too distracting as her time was running out.

After Nana died, I could think of her and conjure the words she would say in any situation (it always ended with 'See, so there'). Lew had passed with many of his secrets intact, we only uncovered a few – who knew his middle name was Wolf? – along with the freezer full of poppers and chicken stock he made in the early '80s.

I still had questions for my mother. She knew I was trying to extract every bit of knowledge she possessed and she was patient with me, complicit in the act. I was trying to memorise my mother, I was trying to store her up. But 'momness' is like sleep and it can't be bottled for later use.

Simon's father died on 18 September 2009, Dexter's first day of school. The call came as we were walking out of the door. My mother's email from later that day said, 'So very sorry to hear the news. All condolences to Nancy and children. You are much in our thoughts.' She didn't need to write 'I'll probably be next.' It seemed like every bit of news we had was draped in death, even good news was shrouded as if written on black-bordered, Victorian mourning stationery.

By late October 2009, the bedroom, living and dining rooms of my parents' apartment had been taken over by medical equipment: oxygen tanks, distilled water, a hospital bed. Do Not Resuscitate orders had been taped to the walls and both the bathroom and bedroom doors alternating with 'Live

Oxygen Do Not Smoke' signs. The writing was literally on the walls.

My father used my presence that weekend to raise the difficult subject of scheduling hospice care, hoping we might make some headway as a double-act but each time we mentioned the word 'hospice', she became breathless and needed the oxygen and more morphine. I finally resorted to typing up a letter and printing it out for her to read. She was able to read it without any extra morphine.

'I'll think about it,' she said in her non-committal way, and then, 'before I forget, Donna, I have something for you.' It was Nana's gold necklace that she had held back four years earlier.

'One last question: so you're sure that I wasn't yours and Leah and Paul were adopted?' My deep-seated fantasy finally spilling forth.

'Aww . . . sorry, no,' she said with a rueful smile.

By the time I left on Sunday afternoon, the accumulated morphine had befuddled her. Dad went ahead and scheduled hospice care but before they had a chance to start, that Thursday, when she was napping, he took a bath and she slipped away.

At first, because she looked so peaceful, he thought she was asleep. I pictured him bending over her, one hand holding the towel around his middle, the other gently shaking her. 'Ruth? Ruth, did you die?'

'She looks so peaceful,' Mom's friend Kala said. She had come over to be with Dad when he called to tell us. 'She looks so peaceful,' he echoed.

After the call, Simon helped me make soup as fireworks exploded around us. It was the fifth of November, Guy Fawkes, Bonfire Night and the whizz bang of local fireworks displays shuddered the windows building to a gunfire spray of sparkling finales. No matter how mindfully I cooked, I could not bring her back this time, but I needed the movements to anchor me as my heart had imploded.

Dad called the next day to ask, 'do you want to see her? If you do, you better get here quick.' Unanimously, we all declined so without telling us, he took pictures of my mother in her final rest and emailed them to us with no subject line or warning of any kind. There are nine pictures, all close ups of her death-flattened face, tinged yellow. She is wearing one of the 'A Star Is Born' t-shirts Uncle Lewis had made for Dad's 75th birthday family reunion, its blue star faded almost to grey.

He mailed hard copies of the photographs, which arrived, also unmarked. I could not and still cannot bring myself to throw them out. I feel a fresh stab of revulsion and sorrow every time I stumble across them.

Mom had died and I was free-floating again, just like the first time I lost her, when I was six and I was no longer hers. But I had become hers and she mine, we had made it so.

I thought I had asked her everything but the day after she died, I had more questions, a torrent of questions, a lifetime of questions that would never now be asked or answered.

I knew all I needed to know about Mom and Dad's conception issues; regardless of whether it was Ruth or Sy, the problem of conception lay between the two of them. And I didn't need to ask Mom why she adopted us in the first place, she did want and love children. She had gotten lost along the way but had eventually found her way back to that love.

I needed her to be alive to answer the question that I asked over and again in my mind and I needed answered over and again. What would you do if you had been better? How do I unlearn who you taught me to be? How can I undo the past? How do I mother Dexter the way you would now and not the way you mothered me? And what happens when I fuck up? How do I unfuck it up? How can I bypass the bad you and go straight to the better you?

The shadow of her early parenting darkened my insides, choking me with night-blooming weeds that self-seeded doubt. It was the living mother who I asked for guidance and that dark stain would deepen in her absence. My mirror had cracked from side to side.

I kept my date with my friend Alegra the next morning. I knew if I could leave the house, even shaky and unsure, Alegra would help steady me. That morning I bought the two most outlandish items of clothing in my already colourful wardrobe. The first was a dress of spring-green tulle, yards and yards of the stuff, embroidered with intertwined passion flowers in white and russet. The second was a high-waisted yellow and blue plaid wool skirt, cut on the bias and asymmetrically ruched creating a deconstructed Victorian silhouette. The bottom of the multi-tiered skirt was bulked out with a crinoline and the final flourish was a floor-skimming electric-blue velvet ruffle. All it lacked was a bustle. I had run away with the grief circus.

I was no longer made in anyone's image. I would wear my grief aloud, my motherlessness like a badge. I would swathe it in bright cloth armour and flaunt it.

During a late-night phone call one week after Mom died, Dad told me that he was planning a trip back to the Outer Banks, to see the tundra swans and other Arctic Circle birds land after their long southerly migrations. It was a trip he had made with Mom ten years earlier when they had first moved south.

'It sounds like a great trip,' I said.

'You want to come?' he asked.

We started out in Belhaven and took the ferry to Ocracoke

Island where we were held up for two extra days by a storm which washed out the road north. We eventually reached Pea Island and from there our final stop was Nag's Head where we were eating dinner at a diner. The waitress had fallen for Dexter's London accent and he was now shadowing her, helping her take orders and bringing water to the tables.

'I've been thinking about what I want for the rest of my life,' my father said. 'I figure I have five or so good years left. I want to travel. Your mother didn't like to travel.'

My father also wanted companionship. 'Life is short. I don't want to get married again but maybe I'll get a girlfriend. I think it's what your mother would have wanted.'

Really? I thought. Ruth? I'm not so sure she would. But undeniably, life is short and rushes relentlessly onward. I would gladly have rushed right past this particular conversation.

'Do you have anyone in mind?' I asked, more to move the conversation forward rather than actual curiosity or an expectation of a name. I thought I would get a 'I'll keep an open mind,' or similar. Instead, he seemed like he'd tallied the plusses and minuses of all the possible candidates in his immediate purview, in other words, my mother's friends. 'Kala's a nice lady, but she speaks too low, I can't hear a word she says.' Gabriela, an Austrian woman and classical music enthusiast was dismissed because she was too old. 'I think she's ninety-three!'

'Maybe Irmgard.'

I spewed my wine all over the table. 'You hate each other!' I managed to wheeze.

'I like a challenge,' he shrugged.

'That's not a challenge, Dad, that's a death wish for both of you!'

On December 27, seven weeks after her death, we held

a memorial concert for Ruth. To celebrate my mother's recovery after the aneurysm and my parents' 50th wedding anniversary four years earlier, my brother, along with colleagues from the New York Philharmonic and the Charleston Symphony, formed the 'Anniversary Quartet' who staged a wonderful, life-affirming concert in the Carol Woods performance hall in December 2006. The concert was such a success that it became an annual event, inked into the calendar on December 27th. The hall was packed and a friend of Paul's composed a new piece inspired by my mother's love of early chamber music.

Mercifully, my father's new girlfriend Sylvia did not sit with us at the memorial and made herself scarce at the reception after the concert.

Sylvia had spied Ruth on her final walk outside and read the clear signs of my father's impending singledom. After Mom died, she held her powder dry for three weeks before sending my father an open and frank letter declaring her interest. 'We like the same things,' he told me over the phone.

He also told me she was wonderful and that he wanted us to meet. 'We'll be there soon for Mom's memorial,' I pointed out. In advance of the meeting, he introduced me over the phone. In what I thought was an accident but proved over time to be purposeful, she hung up when I mentioned Ruth. I promised to meet her for coffee before the memorial.

Although I did not express this to my father, I was horrified and disgusted. Fine if that was what he wanted to do with his life, but could I mourn my mother without him flaunting someone so soon in her place? Did he think that three weeks was so vast an improvement over his own father's 'cavorting' which he had never forgiven him for? At least he waited until Ruth was dead, was that what I was supposed to think? Could I just have some time to think? To mourn without having to grin and bear it and play welcome to the family to Dad's new girlfriend?

It wasn't enough that I had to traipse back and forth to people's deathbeds while trying and failing to be a mother, but now this?

'I came across your father a couple of years ago and kept my eye on him ever since,' she gushed over coffee at Cuppa Joe's.

'It was great, she's great,' I told Dad when I got back.

'I sit in the bath and I cry tears of sadness for Ruth and tears of joy for Sylvia,' Dad says.

After the memorial, we sifted through Mom's books and papers. She had already given away so much that there was very little left of her. Dad had emptied her drawers and closets. Her threadbare thrift shop clothes were easy to part with. Among the remaining papers were lists of Nana and Papa's investments, numerous articles on memory loss (*Is it Memory Loss or Dementia?*, *Memory, Forgetfulness, and Aging: What's Normal and What's Not?*) family relationship charts, menus from Carol Woods along with old residents' handbooks with the deceased residents crossed out and Mom's 'dead' scribbled next to their name; in amongst the flotsam and jetsam, there was an occasional gem.

Dad left the sorting to Leah, Paul and me. We sat with our modest piles in front of us; mine had the *Love and Knishes* cookbook and Nana and Papa's birth certificates. It is with our own brand of dark humour that we 'throw Mom away', tipping the remnants into the dumpster in the dark as the papers slide away. It is late and cold and feels criminal and hilarious, or perhaps, just hysterical.

PART III

Mama Mira

11

DRAMA SCHOOL

We were inhaling fish and chips in Wimbledon after a lengthy and ultimately fruitless trek to the Nissan Figaro dealership to buy our first family car. I was smitten with the diminutive candy-coloured convertibles, but in order to wedge himself into the Lilliputian driver's seat, Simon has to pretzel his legs into a cramped lotus position with his nose abutting the windshield. If these physical challenges weren't enough, the complete lack of a driver's license between us definitively killed the sale.

'Mum, do you have a picture of your other mother?' Dexter asked.

'My other mother?' I packed my mouth with a fistful of chips to avoid answering. I thought he might be referring to my father's girlfriend, Sylvia. The trauma of their abbreviated, springtime visit to London which had started off poorly and gone speeding downhill from there, reaching its nadir with a 2 a.m. call to the police to report Sylvia MIA on the Tottenham Court Road, was still fresh in my mind. We had since discovered that she was experiencing hallucinations possibly associated with Capgras Syndrome, a form of dementia. When we had met them off the Queen Mary, Dexter had sweetly announced, 'You have a new mommy now.'

'No, I don't!' I spat, then quickly tried to disguise my vehement disgust with a laugh and succeeded only in appearing unhinged.

Back in the chippy it hit me: 'Do you mean my birth mother?' He nodded.

I was guarded. 'No, I don't know her, do you want me to look for her?'

'Yes,' he said emphatically, a smile of ketchup contouring his plump cheeks.

I struggled to swallow the wad of sodden potato, my throat suddenly constricted and tears pooled at the corners on my eyes. 'That makes me really miss grandma' I gulped. 'I can look for a picture, sure, but I'm not quite done with my first mother yet.'

'Isn't that other one the first one?' he corrected me.

'Yes, yes I suppose she is. But I think mothers should be enjoyed one at a time.'

'Like biscuits?'

'Yes, like biscuits, exactly.'

The other 'mother who couldn't take care of me' was how I'd framed my adoption for Dexter. It acknowledged the existence of, but no specific knowledge concerning, my adoption. I had first spun this line after he learned a friend of his was adopted, fear of separation and abandonment had shuddered through him, his brows contracted with worry: 'Why couldn't she take care of you?'

'I don't know' was my answer. 'But it's okay that she couldn't, otherwise I wouldn't be who I am now and I might not have you,' I glossed.

Clearly that oblique and philosophical answer sufficed only

for a limited time. Perhaps the high family body count of recent years prompted him to look for reinforcements and my birth mother represented an opportunity to recruit replacements. His question, 'do you have a picture of your other mother' were the magic words, the 'open sesame' required to activate the sleeper agent of my own curiosity.

'You're just looking for this woman because you want a distraction from other problems in your life.' Barbara Miller's dismissive words to my brother chimed inside my head as an automatic reflex, but I thought, yes, yes I most certainly am. And this time, I didn't see any reason why I should suppress it. This was a most welcome distraction and in theory, I wasn't hurting anyone else by looking now.

I had spent so long vociferously denying my interest in looking for my birth family, its folly, the lie at the heart of a search, all bluster to mask its inherent betrayal. At the core of my reluctance was fear. This search was intensely threatening. It had taken me a long, lonely time to come to a point where I liked myself. That struggle for acceptance and confidence helped create the person I thought of as myself. It – I – was something I had fought for and forged myself. I was my own. Ruth hadn't believed it was nature vs. nurture but rather that nurture brought out what nature had created. I agreed to a point, beyond that, as an adult, my own self-determination had provided the finishing touches.

What if I discovered that I was merely a uniform link in some other homogenous family chain. I wouldn't mind looking like someone else but *being* like them was a different proposition. What if everything that I was and thought of as me and mine was merely borrowed, leftover DNA, and not Donna at all?

The timing of Dexter's question was crucial. While Ruth was alive, starting a search for my biological parents wasn't possible. It would have been too conflicting, too insulting to Ruth, too confrontational for me. I couldn't have faced Ruth's disapproval, or worse, disappointment, and looking for my 'other mother' would have been the ultimate act of treachery, tantamount to telling her, after everything I had espoused, that she was not enough, she was not my 'real' mother. To be the person who caused her to feel that would have ripped my guts to pieces. I didn't have the heart to inflict on her the wound that opened up when I was six with the words, 'we were adopted.'

But Dexter's wishing to know about my birth mother allowed me to conveniently sidestep my trepidations. Whatever I uncovered, good or bad, didn't reflect upon me, I was acting as a mother, a mere cipher working on my son's behalf. It upped the ante because I would be disappointing Dexter if I didn't find her. A new urgency for the search awakened in me.

It was apparent that I was a very convincing denier all those years when Simon questioned my motives. I said lofty things to do with my genes and medical history. I had always considered my curiosity superficial in the past, I wondered about aesthetic matters, eye colour or my tiny patellas. The need to know felt like a weakness, slightly craven, but I was also scared of what else I might find, beyond a physical and mental health history. To be met with a terrible or seedy story, tragic circumstances, terror, violence, incest or rape. Would I have automatically inherited my birth parents' trauma?

As long as it wasn't a concrete reality, it could remain amorphous and anonymous, a blank page and mine for the making. I still had choice and power, control over my person and my past, if not the present or future. I was finally stepping beyond the shadow of Ruth's idea of me, I didn't want to walk directly into the shade cast by another parent.

The prospect of rejection lurks behind my reluctance as well. I already felt vulnerable to this unknown mother's judgement. Would I live up to her sacrifice, her gift of adoption? Were my parents worthy of her baby girl? I assumed my successes would be claimed by her and my failures blamed on my parents. I didn't remember that first break from her, that 'primal wound' but I still felt the wrench of the moment when I was knew I was adopted, when I was more or less Dexter's age, the age of questions. The moment I became a separate piece, no longer part of a whole, my questions dried up in my mouth.

Ruth and I had toiled away at our hard-won relationship, we had forged and tended it together and now she was gone and I felt unwitnessed without her. In the same way that it had felt so wrong to move to the UK when she was unconscious, how could I move forward now? I loved having a mom and I felt beyond bereft at her death. As much as I had savoured our relationship, she slipped away. In the void she left, in her wake, as it were, I made room for another mother.

My trepidations were far outgunned by hopeful optimism. What if I found a person who loved me and witnessed my life in the way a mother does? With pride and reverence, but also the ownership and judgement that confers belonging. What if I could have a mom again?

So, eighteen months after Ruth's death, in May 2011, I embraced my inalienable right to curiosity, hiding behind Dexter's untarnished desire to know, which somehow, because he was a child, didn't require justification. I wanted to honour his question, celebrate that he was free to ask. I could let a question be a door, one that I could hold open for him. I didn't want to shut him down because I was scared of the outcome. But I hoped I hadn't waited too long, that my other mother was still alive.

Louise Wise Services was absorbed into Spence-Chapin Services, which also became the court-appointed custodians of their records, in 2004. In lieu of the formidable Barbara Miller, I was assigned to Anne, whose warm, Midwestern singsong of a voice conveyed an earnest efficiency and an honest desire to help.

She took her job as social worker and archivist of family records seriously. She had a fine line to straddle, on the one hand she seemed to want to help me find my family so that I could develop a wonderful lasting relationship, but she wasn't allowed to give me any specifics about that family. Her task was to sketch an outline of my birth circumstances and then, providing both parties had registered their interest, she could orchestrate a reunion.

She began by guiding me through various official forms, presumably the same forms Louise Wise would allegedly fill out on behalf of curious adoptees but never file. I registered with the New York State Adoption Information Registry, which allowed Anne and New York State to release non-identifying information about my birth parents. In the event that my birth mother or father had also registered, I would be notified of the match immediately by Certified U.S. Mail. In the meantime, Anne promised that she would, in accordance with the law, prepare a report for me based on the information provided at the time of my adoption. It would take at least a month as she was obliged to expunge all identifying markers. She would not be able to give me any names but she would describe, in as much detail as she was allowed, how I came to be adopted.

Anne had other reports to prepare before mine but anticipated she'd get to mine around August.

I was in no real rush, I told her; I had waited this long. The train has been set in motion, the die is cast, as Ruth would say, the genie was out and there was no way to re-stopper the bottle. I had embarked on a path that I long denied even existed for me but it is a well-trodden one, pre-plotted, with red tape connecting the dots. In filing my paperwork with the New York State Registry, I was no longer a person who didn't want to know. Apparently, this lady did protest too much.

Summer months drifted by before the fleeting thought 'I wonder what happened,' flickered through and trailed off. My ambivalence was a prophylactic against whatever might be conjured from the cauldron of the past. But it was still more with curiosity than anticipation, that I opened the official looking letter which arrived in late August. Singular among the shiny take-away menus, I assumed the New York State return address signalled tax forms. Flipping it over I saw it was from the Birth Registry.

The single page contained three nuggets of information, three tangible facts. Age of Mother: 27 years; Father not reported, Nationality of Mother: Swiss; Health History of Birth Mother: There were no children born to your mother prior to you.

Swiss? A yodeller? A chocolate-loving banker, a watch-maker? Swiss? Not one of these hackneyed tropes bore any resemblance to me. However, stereotypes aside, this seem-ingly innocuous detail drastically narrowed my search.

According to the *Vital Statistics of the United States* pub-lished in 1939 by the U.S. Department of Commerce with material provided by the Bureau of the Census there were 2,265,588 'consumers' born live in the USA the year of my mother's birth, twenty-seven years before my own live birth in March 1967. In New York State alone there were 187,575 births and if one were to suppose that half of them were female, then 93,787 women could possibly be my mother.

Comparatively speaking, out of the 64,000 births that same year in Switzerland, a mere 32,000 yodelling girls were born and one of those Swiss misses emigrated to the United States and found herself working at the bank, making cuckoo clocks in her spare time and pregnant at twenty-seven, with no prior children to her name and gave birth to me presumably somewhere in New York State. A twenty-seven-year-old American woman could have been anybody, but a twenty-seven-year-old Swiss woman was one in 32,000. Then if you allow for the near certainty that she was Jewish, in 1939, there were 18,000 Jews living in Switzerland, a mere 0.44 % of the population so now that Jewish, twenty-seven-year-old Swiss woman became one in 141! Now that was a figure I could sink my teeth into!

Ethnic background, height, weight, hair and eye colour were all blank. Also unreported were race, skin colour, religion, education and occupation as well as talents, hobbies and interests. All information pertaining to the birth father, Not Reported.

'But Swiss? Really? Me?' I kept pestering Simon.

'It's not so very different from what you thought might be the case: Polish or German, possibly Russian,' he pointed out. These were the combined nationalities of my adopted families and my looks generally echoed that profile.

'Is Swiss too dull for you? Doesn't quite fit the fantasy?' Simon asked, utterly nailing it. And I had to admit that the woman I first fantasised about as my mother, with an ashtray slung round her neck and lounging around on slip-covered furniture didn't seem Swiss to me. European maybe, but not Swiss.

The school year had started by the time I heard back from Anne. After an anxiety ratcheting round of phone tag, we finally connected. She apologised for taking so long to prepare the report but, as she explained, there was a slew of material that she had to work her way through, a much thicker file than usual. 'Before I take you through it,' she cautioned me, 'I need to prepare you for a very dramatic story.'

Clearly, she hadn't met me and neither could she see my expression of exaggerated, eye-rolling exasperation, her gentle sing-song already driving me to inward screeches of impatience. *Please carry on with the story, my story, and I'll let you know when we get to some actual drama!* We were both lucky this meeting was taking place over the phone and not within throttling distance.

'I am going to send you a copy of the report after we've spoken but there's a lot of information here and I wanted to talk you through it first. I want you to know that I really came to like your mother while preparing your file. Are you ready?' the torturous preamble continued.

'Yes,' I spluttered around the fist I had shoved into my mouth to stop the screaming of, 'Come on, woman! So glad you like her, now it's my turn to meet her!'

She started by telling me that my birth mother was born in 1939 in Switzerland. She was twenty-seven-years-old and Jewish, so nothing I didn't already know. She relocated to the United States in her second year of life – so that's when she arrived, 1941!

My Swiss Miss mother stood five foot, eight inches tall; she had blonde hair, grey eyes and an easy, warm laugh. She was described as naturally bright, sensitive and talkative with a wonderful sense of humour. So far, so nice. And tall!

Next Anne told me that my mother was a strong and expert swimmer. The inclusion of this rather random detail struck an odd note. Did she also like pina coladas and getting caught in the rain? Why was she giving me her dating profile and where was the promised drama?

'She lived with her family in a wealthy suburb located in the Northeastern United States until a year before your birth, when she moved to an apartment of her own in a large city . . . she was fluently multi-lingual, well-read and naturally intelligent . . . rose quickly within her place of employ . . . a large advertising agency . . .' Like Anne, I was starting to like this woman too, she sounded rather sophisticated.

Anne's account was a strange mix of the specific and the banal: ' . . .your birth mother's father was sixty-four years old at the time. He was a distinguished looking man, a PhD and a chemist who had emigrated in the employ of a pharmaceutical company . . . His wife, who was born in Latvia but educated in Switzerland was sixty-two at this time. She had worked as a paediatrician but was a housewife in the US. She stood five foot three inches tall and appeared to be devoted to and loyal towards her family. Your birth mother had a sister, thirty-one years of age. She was described as single, a teacher, intense, serious and quiet.'

Like smooth river stones, my mind rushes over these snippets of information but there is nothing to hold on to. There is still nothing to distinguish her from the other 140 young Swiss-born women.

'Now I'm going to tell you about your birth father.' So he was known after all. The ubiquitous 'not reported' from New York State intimated a lack of involvement in the adoption but not involved needn't have meant that he was unknown. It was a scenario that had occurred to me and reignited my fears concerning the circumstances of my conception.

But here was 'the father', my birth father. Assuming the tone of a bed-time story she recounted: 'Your father was a forty-year-old Caucasian, Catholic, married man with four children.' So many lives were bound up in those words, 'married with four children'.

She continued: 'he was handsome, with blue eyes and brown hair.' No mention of curls or lack there of. 'He graduated high school,' she said. 'He was charming, affectionate and charismatic. He had a number of professions, bar tender, jazz musician and construction worker, but according to your birth mother he was a writer and a dreamer . . . but not a man to take his responsibilities seriously.'

Was my birth mother's wry understatement at the moment of giving her child up for adoption indicative of her sense of humour I wondered? Was it his responsibility to her and her child (me) or his wife and four children that he didn't take seriously? But as for drama, this wasn't really pulse-quickening, more the ho-hum workaday stuff of a tawdry affair.

'At the time of your adoption, your father was in jail awaiting sentencing for fraud. He was not permitted to post bail as there were other fraud cases posted against him.'

Hello! A chord of recognition resonated through me, some streak of irreverent wildness, a sense of 'fuck you' that feels familiar in conjunction with their combined intelligence and humour. Fraud had dramatic potential after all. Fraud also embroiled other lives, the accomplices and the marks, the cops and prosecutors. More connections and characters amassed around me, crowding into the story but they appeared like plot points, not (my) flesh and blood people.

Anne pressed on, 'Your parents had an intense three-year relationship. Your mother fell in love with a man thirteen years her senior, and when he asked her to join him in a plan to defraud an insurance company, she agreed in the hopes of securing her relationship with him. Your father told your mother that they could run away together to Spain to live for the rest of their lives if his plan succeeded.'

Aha, finally the drama has entered the building! I sat, like a transfixed carp, my mouth wordlessly opening and closing.

'Your mother left her promising career and her family for this relationship. Your mother said that she was thrilled to have conceived you.'

A breath pushed out of me, directly from my heart. One of the tightly curled fists of fear inhabiting my chest gently unfurled at the knowledge of having been wanted. The idea of me thrilled my birth mother, even if only in that moment, her hand on her belly, looking down in the wonder of what their love had created. 'Pregnant' echoing around her body, filling the contours, breathing love and hope as it swirled through her. Sitting on the side of her bed, dreaming herself into a future filled with love and family. Thrilled about me.

Anne forged ahead, 'However, their plan did not work. Your father was incarcerated and awaiting trial throughout your mother's pregnancy. According to the social record, the court allowed your mother to live at home with her parents until after your delivery when she was expected to stand for sentencing.

Your birth mother was in her eighth month of pregnancy with you when she determined that adoption would be the best and safest plan for you. She arrived for her first interview with her mother. Your maternal grandmother felt strongly that you should be raised in a loving, safe environment, where you could grow up happily. Your mother herself expressed more feelings of ambivalence about planning for adoption; she wanted to raise you, and yet she could not disagree with her mother's common sense about what was in your best interest.'

These were the words that sealed my fate. These were the forces that first came to bear on my story, this was the fork in my road.

'You were born on March 28, 1967 at 12:23 a.m. . . . a full-term baby, by low forceps . . . Your birth mother named you

Rada ... your birth mother was "euphoric" to have and hold you ... you liked to be held tight ... stopped crying when people spoke to you ... you slept through the night almost immediately.'

My birth mother had held me, had named me and been euphoric at doing so.

'Donna, as you know, I can't give you any specific information about the court case itself but the file was full of newspaper clippings. This was a huge scandal and was front page news in all the papers, there was a tremendous amount of publicity.'

'It's a lot to take in,' I gulped.

'I did tell you it was a very dramatic story.' It sounded a tiny bit like 'I told you so.'

'Now I have to ask you, Donna, would you welcome a reunion with your birth mother?'

'Yes, I would!' I shouted, aghast that she even had to ask.

'I'm so glad because she registered her interest in reunion in 1993.'

'I've made her wait so long! Eighteen years!' I choked on sudden tears.

'But she's still alive, right?' my voice was panicky, my throat tight.

'I don't know, but I pray so, Donna. I'll let you know as soon as we make contact.'

My tall, blonde, fool-for-love mother rose to life from the pages of the report. She was bracketed by the shadows of her small, determined mother and her cultured, methodical father. Off to the side, my father did his jail-house shuffle accompanied by a jazz riff, accented with a hi-hat. Far behind him stood the ill-defined grey figures of his wife and children in descending order like Russian dolls. Surrounding all of them is an anonymous jostling crowd of police and prosecutors, judges and social workers, strung round in the rows behind them, the court reporters, crime beat hacks and readers, lapping up all the salacious details.

I searched for evidence of myself in these disjointed fragments of information. I obsessively replayed my mother's joy at my conception, I rocked myself to these words, they were a balm to my soul. It wasn't important whether it was my arrival that thrilled her or if she felt it would anchor my married father to her; in that moment, the moment she knew she was pregnant, she was euphoric. To know that I was welcomed by her soothes and smooths bristles I didn't know were out of place. I was born a product of passion.

I looked up the name Rada, derived from the Slavic element *rad* meaning 'happy or willing'. I laughed at the thought of my mother, both happy and willing – naming me for that time of joy in her life.

Dexter bursts out of his classroom, ready to run riot in the playground. He was in the full thrall to the romance of pirates, the glamour of highwaymen.

'Remember you asked me for a picture of that other mother?'

'Did you get it?' he looked up hopefully.

'No, but I found out a bit about my mother and father . . . your grandfather was in the clinky when I was born!'

'Yes!' he claimed his birth right with a double fist pump and steamed off whooping.

I know one other Rada, a Somali mom at school. 'Rada? It means paradise in Arabic, this is a good name for you, Donna!'

I wait until Simon is home from work to tell him; it would be real when I told him in the way it used to only feel 'real' when I told Ruth.

'So, my name was Rada.' I told him, shy of that name that was me but was no longer me.

'Ah, so you were always a drama queen.'

He saw not only that I didn't understand the non sequitur, but was insulted to boot. 'RADA? The Royal Academy of Dramatic Art?' he explained.

As the days passed and I waited to be reunited with my birth mother, I scoured the report, trying to re-flesh the pale bones, reanimate the traces of DNA. These people I had never met felt familiar, familiar to the point of banal typecast tropes: the upper middle class European parents, the Americanised daughters, the married man. The snapshots of personality that have no names, they are persons of interest but not yet animate people. They were not people I knew, but have the feel of people I had grown up around, distant family, far off relatives.

It was easy to deduce that the big city was New York. I wondered if the advertising agency was Grey Advertising where Uncle Lew once worked and reportedly loathed his job. Had he worked with my mother?

I was proud, in that distant way of legend – like a pioneering past – of my maternal grandmother who had grown up in Latvia, moved to Switzerland, presumably learned a new language and had graduated from medical school. An inspiring immigrant story of opportunity and then, after her arrival in the US, assimilation and motherhood and finally scandal.

I circled my father, trying to get the measure of this bad-boy outsider. I could smell the dangerous smoke of him, his seductive power. I sensed his ghostly hand on my shoulder, egging me on through my teenage years, the author of the wildness that Ruth saw and lured me back from. He was trouble.

My birth mother was harder to grasp. She was obscured by her lover's schemes and her own mother's shadow. I was shy of her. Would she like me? I was going to meet her any day so I could wait for her to come into sharper focus, to reveal her nature and for me to get to know her as her daughter.

Most of all, it was Ruth that I yearned to spend hours with, analysing every detail. Yet, even as I wished it, I knew there were things in the report I would have shielded her from. I wouldn't have told her about that baby who slept through the night, baby Rada. She got baby Donna who cried incessantly through those broken nights, howling and covered in diaper rash, the kind of baby that needed a 'hostile baby-rocking song'.

In Ruth's mute absence, I dreamed myself closer to my birth mother. As I was falling asleep, I thought of her baby, Rada, the daughter she held for seven days before giving her to Louise Wise Services, although she wouldn't sign the adoption papers for another month. That 'bright, alert' baby who hadn't yet experienced the break. She never saw it coming.

'I'm sorry,' Anne says, weeks later, when I could no longer refrain from asking. 'It's proving difficult to locate your birth mother.'

Lost and found and then lost again.

158

12

CALLING ALL ANGELS (2011)

The final paragraph of the background report indicated that my birth mother reached out to the Louise Wise Agency in August 1993. She wanted to let them know, should I enquire, that she was in good health other than the beginnings of macular degeneration, that her mother was still alive and also in good health, that her father had died of pancreatic cancer at the age of seventy and that she had been working for a long time in a bank. The final two sentences read: 'She said she would welcome reunion. She was referred to the NYSAIR (New York State Department of Health Adoption Information Register).'

I giggled about the bank but here, among the free-floating facts were the first indications of the medical history I had professed to want, hereditary markers to watch out for. My grandfather's death at the relatively early age of seventy did not seem of particular significance but it seemed prudent to get my eyes checked.

I thought back to August, 1993 and while I cursed myself for not looking for her sooner, I knew in my bones that it would have been impossible to meet her at that particular time. If that had been our one chance, I would have blown it. I was twenty-six, raw and ragged, slogging through my lowest ever point. My life had been derailed in the aftermath of a sexual assault the month before. At the hospital, I had been asked if I would tell my parents and I immediately said I would. This was not my shame. By that time, I had learned that I did not have to assume the shame and that I was not alone, Ruth would provide the succour I needed. My parents had come to pick me up and had taken me home.

Even from that place of relative safety, getting through to the end of each day was a herculean task and I think I would either have rejected a reunion as too much to take in or take on or I would have seized upon it and smothered it with so much significance that I would have extinguished any possibility of connection.

In 1993, I was the same age as my birth mother when she was pregnant with me, when she embarked upon the adventure that ended not happily-ever-after in Spain, but with her lover in jail and their baby given away. At that same age, Ruth had come to the realisation that she could not get pregnant and would never give birth.

The woman who reached out for reunion in 1993 was fifty-four, an age of taking stock, my age as I write this. The same age that Ruth broke free of her own cage of depression. The three of us unwittingly following in each other's emotional footsteps.

While I was in limbo, waiting for my birth mother to heed my belated desire for reunion, Anne recommended looking up my birth name. Each birth in New York State was recorded and kept in the New York Public Library. The births were grouped by year and listed alphabetically by the mother's last name and cross referenced with a corresponding number from the original birth certificate.

There were numerous online forums advertising 'adoption angels', New Yorkers who were only too happy to trot off to the library to dig through the records on your behalf. Not one angel responded to my calls and more precious time leached by. I recruited my own New Yorker friends, my adoption angels Marcus, Jeffrey and Peter.

In our early twenties in New York, we made easy and fluid friendships. It was a time when friends of friends became friends for life through copious hours of drinking, dancing, biking, cooking, talking, sharing, bitching and moaning, always accompanied by a soundtrack of raucous laughter. These friendships once started, took on a life of their own, and these were friends who took your late-night distress calls and helped you find your mother. I met Marcus through Jeffrey, whom I met through Karen, who was friends with my friend Jill, whom I met through my friend Jennifer, whom I met when I was dating Chris who was friends with her boyfriend Patrick. I met Peter after Chris and I broke up and I dated a guy who he was friends with named Doug. Marcus and Jeffrey met Peter through me.

Jeffrey and Peter were the embodiment of Patience and Fortitude, the two marble lions who flank the steps of the library, as they systematically worked their way through the Index to Live Births, 1866–1982, all boroughs, housed in the Milstein Division on the ground floor. To my shame, I discovered only much later that the Register was available online.

Their packed schedules meant that progress was steady, but slow. Given the time difference, I would generally wake to the news of their finds.

'Regrettably Rada has not yet been found ...'

'I went right to Davis to make sure you weren't Judy Davis' daughter after all!'

'I got all the way through the "D"s ... so you are NOT Rada A., Rada B., Rada C., or Rada D ...' wrote Peter.

They were busy and as I told them, a mother last seen forty-four years earlier was not a priority. Of course it was to me, but I was also three thousand miles away.

Jeffrey reported that pages 103–104 had been torn from the first of two volumes of 1967 births. Some selfish oaf had grabbed evidence of their own birth and so robbed everyone else of the chance to find theirs.

The search captured our collective imaginations. Jeffery was tickled by the lives he saw in the names, they vibrated with drama and possibility. They prophesied destinies, stars plotted in a dramatic arc.

'Your additional (presumably female) birthday mates, same day/same year/same borough from this evening's search are as follows:

Jean Bryer
Mary Caldwell
"Female" Carlson
Elena Chambous
Christina Chang
Sheila Clancy
Jamie Collard
Victory Ducey
and, the award-winning: Stardell Concepcion!

Will return to the mines tomorrow evening. If we don't come up with Rada in the book, I'm calling you Stardell from here on out. Just sayin.'

On the other hand, Peter's doggedness revealed some

potential obstacles: 'I'm back at the library doing the search for Rada. But me being the contrary pisser that I am, have found some possible roadblocks. First for the searchers – that means you Jeff. The number we're looking for will be the last four digits of the birth certificate.

Also for you Donna, we need to know when and where your adoption was filed, i.e.: if your adoption took place in Westchester then you may not be registered here in NYC. I've checked for your adoptive birth certificate, which should be here, however, you are not. I checked 1967 through 1972. If you know the name of the adoption agency we could find out where they might have filed . . . But I will of course still look for Rada.'

This might indeed have proved problematic as my birth certificate lists Ruth and Sy as my parents and its number might not be the original number issued at birth but a new one, generated at the time and for the purposes of my adoption. These new birth certificates were a re-writing of birth histories and some kept the original certificate number, while others were issued with a new one, expunging the original record.

But to my relief, Anne's background detailed that I was born at 12:23 a.m. on March 28, 1967 and I left the hospital – and my birth mother – on April 4, seven days old, to board with Louise Wise foster parents. My birth mother agreed to my adoption on April 27.

My birth certificate was dated a year later, on April 24, 1968 and listed New York Hospital in Manhattan as my place of birth, and the exact same time of birth and my parents address in Flushing, Queens – so definitely all still in New York, New York. I should be in those books somewhere and it better not be on pages 103 or 104.

Jeffrey battled through the Is and Js to no avail.

I was not immune to their flights of fancy, but I was cocooned, almost defensively, in a fantasy of my own. Finding and having a mother again, seemed like the perfect antidote to having lost a mother. It felt less like a diversion from my grief and more like a sanctioned quest. An eye for an eye, a mother for a mother.

My guiding thought, the assurance that I clung to with almost religious zeal, was that I would find a mother who would shower me with maternal love. I did not say this to my brother or sister. In the context of our adoptions and our individual experiences of Ruth, it felt like bragging. The love we had from Ruth was a shared and finite resource that we had to parcel out amongst ourselves, a zero-sum game, like Halloween candy, we jealously guarded our stash while eyeing up each other's. This mother's love, my mother's, I would have all to myself, I would be the sole focus of her love. I entertained no other possibility.

Perhaps, Ruth would have eventually filled in the gaps of my need for maternal love if she had lived longer but those gaps remained and had yawned open since her death. I pinned all my hopes and needs on my birth mother; I was a fool for love just like the birth mother I was about to meet.

On Tuesday, November 22, my angel Peter's persistence finally paid off.

'I believe I have uncovered the elusive Rada, Last name Lindenmaier – a mouthful. First name ... sorry Donna, "Female". But that's common in adoption cases. Girl! You owe me enough hair products for a year. Lol. Call when you wake up. Next step finding mama. love you, Peter.'

My certitude in my mother's love only grew with knowing my name. She had named me for joy. She had named me by herself and for herself. She had named me to mark herself onto me. She had given me this name, knowing I would not keep it, that this name, her name for me, would be hers alone to say. She laid what claim she could during the short time of her influence.

I returned to the report: 'The Louise Wise social worker went to the hospital to visit you and your birth mother. She said that your birth mother was "euphoric" to have and hold you, and that she was "thrilled, devoted and involved" in caring for you in the hospital.'

In a room at New York Hospital, from March 28 to April 4, 1967, I was Rada Lindenmaier and I slept in my mother's arms.

The power to name someone or something denotes a proprietary relationship, that you are the discoverer, inventor, progenitor of something or someone, be it a comet, a syndrome, a machine, a baby, a pet or a disease. The act of naming is an act of association and ownership. 'You gotta name it to claim it,' as Dr Phil and Oprah espouse. Paul, Leah and I all came with names that Ruth and Sy didn't know and weren't told; but it fell within their rights to rename us.

My name is Donna Freed but I was born Rada Lindenmaier. My name suddenly felt like a stage name that I hadn't chosen. Would my name have shaped me differently? I stuck out enough growing up with the odd ball Freeds, so I couldn't imagine that being called Rada instead of Donna would have made that much of a difference. What's in a name? Would a Donna by the name of Rada smell as sweet?

Did Ruth feel like an imposter when her parents changed their name to Bolan? She assumed her husband's name when she took up the mantle of marriage, but did she feel like a Bolanski or a Bolan or a Freed?

Now that Peter had the name, the chase quickened. He found no Lindenmaiers born in 1939 on the Death Registry. When he reported this, I was merely relieved that my mother was most likely alive. I did not immediately grasp the possi-bilities of the Death Registry, but it obviously penetrated my subconscious where it percolated until I awoke in the middle of the night with the sudden realisation that I knew the ages and therefore birth years of my maternal grandparents and I also now knew their last name.

'Your birth mother's father was sixty-four years old at this time ... her father died of pancreatic cancer at the age of seventy.' Birth and death.

And lo and behold, lurking in the Death Registry were my grandparents. One Werner Lindenmaier was born December 4, 1903 and died May 18, 1973 in Essex County, New Jersey and a Braina Lindenmaier was born August 2, 1905 and died April 2, 1998 also in Essex County, New Jersey. They lie side by side, tucked together in the Registry.

I thought of these names, left untouched and intact through immigration. Had they come through Ellis Island in the late 1800s or early 1900s their name would have been simplified, Lindenmeyer, Lindenmayer or perhaps even chopped in half to Linden or Meyer. But in 1941 the Lindenmaiers uprooted themselves from Switzerland, when, as the background report stated, they emigrated with the pharmaceutical company that employed Werner. The same time as one Peter Neubauer – future author of the nature vs. nurture study of twins and triplets – also set sail from Switzerland to seek his fortunes in America, never knowing their paths would cross through Louise Wise Services.

Simon stepped through the door the moment after I put the words 'Lindenmaier', 'defraud' and 'insurance' into a google search.

'Bingo' I shouted, 'I found her!' and the articles cascaded down the page.

I read out loud from the first article I clicked on at random:

'A twenty-seven-year-old woman research analyst, reported dead five months ago, has been found alive in what authorities describe as a bizarre plot by her and two male companions to defraud two insurance companies by staging her accidental drowning.

'Dr. and Mrs. Werner A. Lindenmaier of Upper Montclair, NJ . . .'

'I know people who live in Upper Montclair!' I exclaimed, slapping at Simon's arm.

' . . .had not known that their daughter, Miriam, was alive until they were reunited with her Tuesday in the Bronx County courthouse.

'Miss Lindenmaier was found working as a waitress for 87 cents an hour and tips in a restaurant in White Plains, NY . . .'

'I grew up in White Plains!'

'She was arrested Tuesday in her hotel room. One of the accused men, Alvin Brodie, forty, a construction worker named by authorities as the father of Miss Lindemaier's unborn child, was alleged to have promised her that they could go to Spain with the $36,000 in insurance money . . . Roberts said Miss Lindenmaier, a 5-foot, 6-inch blonde is six months pregnant.'

'With me!'

'Authorities said Brodie resides with his wife and four children.

'Brodie was arraigned Tuesday night in Bronx Criminal Court and charged with attempted grand larceny and conspiracy by "staging the accidental death" of Miss Lindenmaier last July 9 in Long Island Sound.

'Miss Lindenmaier was paroled in custody of her parents. Brodie was ordered held on $7,500 bail.'

'So that's why the report said she was a strong swimmer!'

The article was from *The Aberdeen Daily News*, December

14, 1966, although there were scores of column inches devoted to it in *The New York Times* and all the national papers as well as the local papers in each state, it made international news in Canada, Australia and *ABC* in Spain, '*La analista Miriam Lindenmaier . . .*'.

As it turns out, I wasn't the only one who had googled this story. On another computer, another woman had put in some of the same words into a search long before I did, with the same results. Hers started out as an idle search using her grandmother's name and she was shocked to see her aunt's criminal past exposed, a story she had never been told. She wondered what had become of the baby Mira carried. She wouldn't find out until 2020.

My cheekbones protruded from beneath Miriam's sunglasses as she was driven to her arraignment. In a photograph from the *New York Times*, the swell of me is visible beneath her thick coat. Braina and Werner looked shocked, rigid in their courtroom seats, fixed in an aspic of grief and wonder at their daughter's spectacular and very public return from the dead. Brainaw as the very image of my 8th grade school photo, but wrinkled with time and worry at sixty-two.

Stock Getty photos show my bespectacled mother on the steps of the Bronx County Courthouse, carefully picking her myopic way down the stairs, a policewoman at her side. I gasped at the next photo, unable to tell whether I was looking at the past or my future. Alvin Brodie, sporting a goatee, is handsome and collected in a pristine, camel-hair overcoat, his arms pinned behind him, as he is led down the same steps by two schlumpy-looking detectives in creased trousers and rumpled shirts. He is Dexter with a beard, or will be or could be. Our faces leapfrog through the generations.

The reports wound their way through the AP and UPI wires to newspapers far and wide, steaming with sex and scandal and scorn. The drowned-and-presumed-dead blonde bombshell and her handsome rogue of a lover to whom she had given a $2,300 Jaguar as a present schemed for a glamorous get-away and instead the gritty, grounded detective found the Jezebel, pregnant and disgraced, in a fleabag hotel serving coffee to the cops for 87 cents an hour.

The reports are lurid, casting my mother as a femme fatale. Alvin's wife was the hapless drudge, drowning in children and grey porridge, my father was the no-good grifter and his accomplice was a rube and a dupe. I sensed the editorial hand of Anne when she recreated my redacted background and I wondered how much of my report she had paraphrased from the papers; the details of the woman featured in these reports were no clearer, only the details of the crime. I couldn't tell if she was 5 foot 6 inches or 8 inches. Taken as a whole, I could piece together a composite picture, plot the whereabouts of the perpetrators, place them in a timeline. The exact implications of that timeline did not occur to me during this first full-on flood of information.

My mother was first reported missing in the July 10, 1966 edition of the *New York Times*. 'Woman Missing in Sound' They report that Mira Lindenmaier went missing the previous day in the Long Island Sound between City and Hart Islands, in the Bronx, when the 14-foot outboard motorboat she and two male companions were travelling in, overturned. Her companions, both of 1825 First Avenue, were listed as Alvin Brodie, thirty-four, and Thomas Martin, twenty-four. The men were picked up by an off-duty detective in his own boat. They said they had thought Miss Lindenmaier was a good swimmer. The detective, Barth Jacobello, saw the men swimming. The boat apparently capsized around 5:30 p.m. and the search for Mira began forty minutes later.

How the editors must have delighted in writing the

headlines: '"Dead" Woman Found Alive To Foil Insurance Fraud' from the *Times Colonist* in Victoria, Canada; 'July "Drowning Victim" Back As Police Dredge Up a Plot' from the *Press and Sun Bulletin*, Binghampton, NY; 'Police Put Damper On "Drowning" Plot, Wiretaps Bring Girl "Back to Life"' from Atlanta, Georgia; and my favourite, NY Times News Service: 'Drowning Story Didn't Hold Water, Three Face Charges.'

The *New York Post*, the *Daily News* and the *New York Times* delved into the grubby details of this local story. The *Daily News* focuses on my mother, the supposed victim turned temptress and dubs her the 'Double Indemnity Girl'. 'Friends Cite the Double Life of a Double Indemnity Girl', 'Double-Indemnity Love: Career girl's strange fadeout bares larceny motive in her romance.' The *Daily News* and the *New York Times* reference the famous Theodore Dreiser novel: '"Victim" Found Alive: An American Tragedy with a Bronx Twist', and 'A New American Tragedy Has Arresting Ending for Three' from the *Daily News*.

An American Tragedy was Dreiser's 1925 fictional account of the tragic plight of Grace Brown. Grace was an upstate New York's farmer's daughter who went to work at the Gillette Skirt Company in Cortland, New York in 1904 where she met the owner's nephew, Chester Gillette. In 1906 her drowned and pregnant body and an upturned boat were found in Big Moose Lake in the Adirondack Mountains where Chester had lured her with the promise of marriage. Chester Gillette was later executed for her murder.

The novel was further popularised by the film, *A Place in the Sun* (1951) directed by George Stevens, featuring, as the trailer gushed, 'Flaming Young Stars' Montgomery Clift, Elizabeth Taylor and Shelley Winters as Grace Brown, which won six Oscars. More recently, the story was retold in Jennifer

Donnelly's young adult novel, *A Northern Light* (or *A Gathering Light* in the UK where it won the 2003 Carnegie Medal).

Some papers surmised the torrid tale was the inspiration for Alvin's half-baked scheme. The detective in charge, Detective Edward Dermody, smelled a rat from the get-go. He was a veteran fisherman who knew the vessel they had rented – 'an outboard dory-type skiff' – was highly unlikely to capsize. When there was no sign of a body despite searches by police launches, helicopter surveillance and dredging of the water by police and the Coast Guard, he suspected homicide. His hunch was re-enforced by reports – from both her companions and her father – that Mira was a strong swimmer. He said he also suspected that Mira, like Grace Brown, might have been pregnant and that might well have been Alvin's motive for murder.

In an article reprising the saga dated 1991, Dermody remembered visiting Mira's apartment with Werner and Braina Lindenmaier after she had been reported drowned. '"Where are her clothes?" her father demanded. "There are only a handful of things here. If she drowned, everything she owned would be here except the clothes she wore."'

Dermody must have thought of Grace Brown's fully packed suitcase when she left for the Adirondacks to meet her lover. He went in search of answers to Mira's workplace, the Madison Avenue advertising agency Metropolitan Sunday Newspapers, Inc. where she had worked for over six years as a media and rates analyst earning $5,500 per year. There, Dermody found 'a woman Mira had confided in a little more than other workers.'

'She [Mira] told me Brodie was witty and had a good sense of humour and made her feel comfortable and good' this woman told the lawyers. 'And from something she said, I got the idea that maybe she was a little pregnant.'

Detective Steve Brenner was assigned to work with Dermody on the case. The nature of the investigation changed abruptly when the cops learned that Mira had two life insurance policies, one for $10,000 with the Metropolitan Life Insurance Co and the other for $8,000 with the Equitable Life Assurance Society. They both carried double indemnity clauses and would have yielded a total of $36,000 in the case of accidental death. Miriam, or Mira, Lindenmaier had changed the beneficiary on both policies from her father, Werner, to Alvin Brodie a mere thirty-nine days before her drowning. This was now quite clearly a conspiracy.

In September 1966 Alvin Brodie attempted to collect on the insurance payout from Equitable Life. This premature move succeeded only in ratcheting up the case against the conspirators. Assistant District Attorney John Breslin joined the investigation and an order for a wire-tap was granted by Supreme Court Justice Mitchell Schweitzer, presumably on Alvin Brodie's phone. The wire-tap bore fruit on Thanksgiving Day, November 24, 1966 when they first heard Mira's voice. They traced her to the Westchester Hotel Court at 22 Tarrytown Road, White Plains, New York where she was registered under the name of Elizabeth Pangborn.

Detectives were dispatched the 18 miles north to White Plains where they showed Mira's photograph – presumably supplied by her mourning and distraught parents – to the local investigators who recognised their waitress from nearby Schrafft's; the cops rushed to the restaurant to see for themselves. Mira poured them coffee, none the wiser as they clocked that the 'tall, attractive blonde' was somewhat thick around the middle and afterwards placed her under surveillance as she traipsed back and forth between the hotel and Schrafft's to work her shifts. On the morning of 13 December 1966, they arrested Miriam Lindenmaier, also known as

Mira, at the hotel. She immediately confessed and signed a waiver of immunity.

Without a word of explanation, her parents were summoned to the Bronx Country Courthouse. The *New York Times* reported that Mira, 'who is twenty-seven years old, and reportedly six months pregnant, was reunited briefly with her parents and then whisked off with her two men companions to be arraigned on charges that the three had plotted to defraud two insurance companies of $36,000.' The trio were charged with violating Section 1202 of the Penal Law (Grand Larceny), a felony, and violating Section 580 of the Penal Law (Conspiracy), a misdemeanour. When she stood to hear the charges of conspiracy to commit grand larceny and attempted grand larceny, Werner and Braina stood with her.

Alvin Brodie and Thomas Martin were held on $7,500 bail each and Mira was sent home in the custody of her parents. The 1991 *Daily News* story states that all three were indicted and pled guilty on 16 March 1967 but the court records show that it was on the 15th, the unlucky Ides of March, two weeks before she gave birth to me.

In the photographs, Mira and Alvin, Werner and Braina, all averted their eyes downward, away from the cameras. Only Thomas Martin looks out blankly at photographers from the back of a police car, his gaze level, thin strands of hair grazing his high forehead.

Speaking to reporters after the arraignment, Chief Assistant District Attorney, Burton B. Roberts again evoked the Theodore Dreiser novel, calling the case '*An American Tragedy* with a Bronx twist.' He repeated a statement that he had made during the arraignment and that would be used in later court proceedings; he said that the case would not have been solved without the use of the judge-approved wire-tap. Without it, he said, 'this girl could not, as far as her folks are concerned, have been raised from the dead and returned to her father and mother.'

On behalf of District Attorney Isidore Dollinger, Roberts also declared that the police were still looking for a third man who allegedly collected Mira from the scene of the capsizing in a motorboat and drove her to safety.

Alvin Brodie and Thomas Martin were sentenced to three years in prison by Supreme Court Justice Joseph A. Brust. Mira Lindenmaier also received a three-year sentence but the term was suspended and she was placed on probation. Martin's sentence was also suspended and only Alvin, the man with the plan and priors, served time.

The twist of course, in this American tragedy, was that instead of being the wronged innocent who drowned with her unborn baby, my mother had bobbed up, alive and unharmed and pregnant as hell, and so was then re-cast as the deceitful, mantrap witch. The blanket news coverage was to be her public pillory, her burning shame.

I gorged on these details as eagerly as any reader must have done in 1966. I wondered if my parents had read this story. Could it have been the very *New York Times* that my sister was paging through during that fateful visit from the social worker?

I stared at my grandparents, Werner and Braina Lindenmaier, a chemist and a retired paediatrician respectively. The *New York Times* quoted 'the tall, distinguished-looking' Werner: '"We never gave up hope." In a soft, heavily accented voice, the father said, "We're glad to have Mira back."' Some reports indicated that a suspicious and disbelieving Werner had wanted to offer a reward for information about his 'big, healthy girl, a strong swimmer' but Detective Dermody vetoed the idea as he didn't want to spook his suspects. My grandmother embodied the 'joy and sadness' attributed to the occasion. The shock of Mira's resurrection coloured by her arrest, her participation in this outlandish plot and her willingness to let them believe she was dead and flee to Spain. And then, on top of all that, there was the no small matter of her pregnancy. But at least she was alive and given time, all this too would pass.

I was intrigued about Mira and Alvin's known accomplice, Thomas Martin, who was described only as an elevator operator and a neighbour of Alvin's. He was found clinging to the remains of the boat they had hired at Jack and Sal's City Island boatyard. So caught up in playing his role in the caper that he had to be forcibly convinced to stop his desperate diving for Mira and get into the off-duty detective's boat. Why did he go along with the doomed escapade? Was he caught up in the romance and excitement or was he simply promised a healthy cut of the money?

Alvin himself swaggers through the words, dabbling in construction work here, jazz music there but always the debonair flaneur. It seemed more likely to me that my 'poetic' father was more influenced by the film *Double Indemnity* (1944) than *An American Tragedy*. Why would he have settled for $18,000 when the insurance policy would have paid double for an accidental death? That $36,000 would be roughly $300,000 today, certainly enough to start a new life in Spain if that was truly ever his plan.

There were contradictory reports in the press coverage about Alvin, his age was said to be both thirty-four and forty. His address is either at 1825 First Avenue, along with Thomas Martin's or at 340 East 92nd Street (both addresses were a short, five-minute walk around the corner from Mira at 328 East 90th Street). At the time of the fateful incident, Alvin was alternately swimming when the off-duty detective chanced upon them or clinging to the upturned boat, unable

175

to swim while Thomas Martin frantically dived to look for Mira. Everything I have found out since leads me to believe that Alvin was as slippery a fish as ever there was and perfectly capable of lying about his age, his address and anything else when it suited him.

Mira met the married, father of four in a 'taproom.' I could smell the smoke and see the polished floorboards underfoot and Mira's wavy, blonde hair in a spotlight as she leaned in to hear Alvin's silver-tongued sweet nothings, his hot breath sending goose pimples shivering down her neck. Reading about Alvin and Mira felt like snooping through your parent's love letters. An invasion of privacy, yes, but as the fruit of their liaison, something I felt privy to even without their consent.

More than anyone, my head was filled with thoughts of this 'fluently multi-lingual, well-read and naturally intelligent' woman who was game to leave everything behind and start afresh, in Spain, with her lover and their baby. It was easy to see why Anne, when preparing the background report, 'grew to like' Mira. I was smitten and had already become protective of her. I wondered why she or they chose White Plains? I puzzled over the possible significance of the name Elizabeth Pangborn, was this some obscure literary reference? I wondered how they were planning to get to Spain, there was no mention in the papers of a plan. Just Spain, no city, just the country, like their fingers happened to stop there on a spinning globe.

The Westchester Hotel Court at 22 Tarrytown Road was all of five minutes away from the house where I lived from the age of three. I must have walked in her footsteps countless times as she made her way to 193–195 Main Street to work at Schrafft's.

I pictured her leaving the Bronx on the local train to White

Plains and checking in as Elizabeth Pangborn, trying it out in the real world for the first time. She must have known when Alvin was planning to claim the money. The months ticked by as she went from the hotel to Schrafft's, from Schrafft's back to the hotel, growing heavier with each passing week. When she could take it no longer, when the rest of the country was celebrating with family, lonely and in need of assurance, she broke protocol and picked up the phone. Just a lone voice on a wire-tap from a young woman, marooned, alone and pregnant on Thanksgiving Day wondering when Alvin would come for her. 'When are you coming?

The Death Registry wasn't done spilling its secrets. Alvin J. Brodie, born January 29, 1932, died on July 14, 2004 in New York, New York 10003. At the time of his death, he had been living for some time in the East Village, a hop and a skip on the subway away from me in Brooklyn. I had also walked in his shadow. He died when I was three months pregnant with Dexter and a year before we left New York for London. How many times did I pass his door? A door I would never enter.

Twenty-five years after the initial events and incidentally on Ruth's 59th birthday, Sunday, 22, September 1991, the *Daily News'* 'Justice Story', with their 'exclusive take on true crime tales of murder, mystery and mayhem for nearly 100 years' reprised the story of Alvin, Mira and Thomas Martin as told from the perspective of Detective Dermody. The final sentence of the article (*SOGGY CHARADE – THE JUSTICE STORY*) reads, 'After her baby was born it was placed for adoption.'

When that story was published, I was working in the research department of *Good Morning America* where one of our tasks was to go through the newspapers, local and national, including the *Daily News*, for topical stories or potential human-interest stories. I wonder if I would read the article.

Two years after that article was published, Mira had reached out to me, but where was she now?

13

HAPPY HANUKKAH (2011)

The story of my parents' escapade faded from the foreign press relatively quickly, but the local papers continued to give column inches to the story weeks after the case concluded. 'Donna, you're the most famous person I know and you weren't even born yet!' Jeffrey said when he saw the *New York Times* articles.

In the *Daily News* and the *New York Post*, Mira's friends and co-workers were called upon to comment and she was invariably described as 'smart, funny and quiet'. 'Sounds like you except the quiet part!' my friends agreed.

I tamped down the sting of losing Alvin before I even had a chance to meet him with the salve of tracking down Mira. My adept adoption angels remained on the case and she couldn't hide forever.

Peter suggested an intriguing possibility. 'I bet she's collecting Social Security. If you have her social security number you could send them a letter to see if she's dead or not. My mother did that when looking for my wayward father. She told them that she had heard he was dead and that she had

179

children and didn't want to tell us until she could confirm his death. They offered to forward a letter as they could not give his address. Trust! He was quite indignant about being thought of as dead.'

'So, he was fine with being a deadbeat dad, just not dead! Peter, you may have missed your calling,' I told him, 'you're very good at this, it's a little scary.'

Peter persisted, 'Hey sweets, if you have a SS number and if your mother has a middle name we can do a search across insurance policy databases to see if she has any kind of coverage.'

'LOL, Peter is supposing that your mother was ever allowed to purchase insurance again!!!' Jeffrey joked. But alas, I had none of that information, only those details the newspapers saw fit to print.

Marcus hadn't been able to visit the library but on December 9, he forwarded a screen grab from a public records website which listed recent addresses and a phone number for Miriam Lindenmaier in Fort Lauderdale, Florida and an older one in Montclair, New Jersey. Before he pressed send, he dialled the number.

'What were you going to say?' I jumped in. I didn't want to appear ungrateful but that was my call to make. I would not repeat my brother's 'it's not my story.' My mother was my story.

'Don't worry, if anyone picked up, I was going to ask, is Rose there?' he assuaged my fears. 'The number was out of order, though.'

By the time I woke up the following morning, there was an email from Peter with a link to a Broward County Sheriff's Jobs Forum from 1998. The post was an informative response to a question about Police Academy exam schedules; it was signed off by the manager, Brenda, as well as two employees, one of whom was Mira Lindenmaier.

'How could she work at the sheriff's department, didn't she have a police record?' Jeffrey asked.

Over the weekend, after Simon and Dexter fell asleep, I spent the nights scrolling through the voicemail options of the Broward County Sheriff's Office: If you want Bob Smith, please press extension 451 ... if you want ... I finally hear what I'm waiting for in the early hours of Monday morning: If you want Brenda D press...'

Instead of calling, I carefully noted the extension number. I had to wait until I could think of something more discreet than a bullish 'Do you know my mother? Tell me where she is!' I also had to convey my sense of desperate urgency without causing undue alarm or suspicion. By the next day, I had settled on: Hi Brenda, I'm a relative of Mira Lindenmaier's and I'm trying to get in touch with her. I live in England so if you can help or if you have any information, maybe you could email me.' I painstakingly enunciated the spelling of my email address three times and thanked her in advance for her help.

It was after 8 p.m. London-time when Brenda got back to me, 'Mondays are busy at the academy.' According to her co-worker, Mira was at the Hollywood Nursing Center and she provided a phone number. I had no way of knowing if it was a main number with a receptionist or a direct line. I could have googled the facility and checked but I could also just take my chances and make the call.

At that moment, I wished I had a Bakelite dialler and an old-fashioned rotary phone so I could have whipped around each number, letting the dial slick back into place before whipping round the next. There was less sense of occasion in pressing buttons on the cordless phone, but then the connection broke the hiss and there was the change in tone before the phone rang once ... twice...

'Hello?' the voice was deep.

'Hello, I'd like to speak with Mira Lindenmaier?'

'This is she.' My heart thudded with the confirmation and swelled at the proper grammar. I hesitated.

'I have some rather big news for you, is that okay?'

'That depends, I guess,' and she laughed. A deep, easy chuckle. Good grammar and she's funny! I took a deep breath in.

'I was born on March 28 . . .' her gasp almost sucked away my words.

' . . .1967 and my name was Rada Lindenmaier . . .'

'Oh!' she cried and I was crying too.

'Does that mean anything to you?' I croaked, both of us were sobbing loudly.

'It's you, it's really you!'

'And it's you!' I answered her.

'It's a Hanukkah miracle!'

The traditional Hanukkah blessings offer praise to our God, Ruler of the Universe, who makes us holy through His commandments, and commands us to kindle the Hanukkah lights and who performed miracles for our ancestors in their days at this season.

But on the first night of Hanukkah there is an additional prayer: Blessed are you, our God, Ruler of the Universe, for giving us life, for sustaining us, and for enabling us to reach this season.

I was not too late.

'My name is Donna now,' I introduced myself.

'Hello, Donna!' she crowed her welcome.

'Are you Mira or Miriam?'

'Mira, I was always Mira. They had to call me Miriam on my birth certificate because Mira isn't a Swiss name and they only allowed Swiss names, so I was Miriam.' One of the many small mysteries explained.

In the rush and gush of our first tumble of words I let slip that Alvin had died in 2004.

'Oh, so much information at once,' she saddened.

'I'm so sorry, I thought you would have known.'

'We lost track of each other over the years, but I liked to think of him out there somewhere.'

Alvin wasn't a picture in the paper, the cartoon seducer and villain to her; he was her flesh and blood everything at one point. Like Oedipus, I arrived back in my mother's life on the heels of my father's death.

'I'm sorry to spring all this on you but I just got the number from your old boss Brenda and I didn't want to wait another minute before meeting you.'

'It's been too long already!'

'I'm so glad I found you,' I tell her.

'Me too.'

'I've only seen pictures of you from the papers.'

'Oh god.'

'I think I look a bit like you, I have cheekbones like yours,' I said shyly.

'Oh really?' I recognised the surprised catch in her throat. Picturing me was either impossible or emotionally off limits. I could almost feel her hand caress her own cheek.

I had studied her on paper like a school project, scouring the pictures and fragments of her life that I had assembled. Naturally, I knew much more of her than she did of me. 'It definitely looks like I got my eyebags from Alvin though,' I said, laughing. 'The report that the adoption agency gave me said you have grey eyes, but they didn't say anything about Alvin's.'

'He had bright blue eyes,' she said slowly, remembering.

'I must have got his eyes too. Your grandson, Dexter, also has the same eyes.'

'My grandson!?'

I gave her a potted history of my doings for the last forty-four years. I told her that Ruth died but that Seymour is still alive. 'My mother died too,' she tells me. 'I'm sorry I didn't meet her,' I say. I was cautious about revealing too much of my early family life; it felt safer to talk about my family now, the family that is hers too, her son-in-law and her grandson.

Eager to forge our connections, I trotted out the moments where our paths had crossed: 'You know, I grew up in White Plains and I know people in Upper Montclair, New Jersey. My brother's friends the Fishes grew up there.'

'I knew a Selma Fish,' she said.

'That's their mom! How have we never run into each other with all these coincidences?'

'Maybe we did?'

There was a pause, as the gravity of all that lost time sank in.

'I know you looked for me a while ago. I'm sorry, I didn't know that until recently,' I said.

'That's okay, you're here now.'

'I've been trying to find you since September, the agency was looking as well.'

'Oh yeah, there was a letter from my lawyer about it,' she said a bit vaguely.

She told me that she was currently resident in the Hollywood Rehab Center. She had gone in with a hip problem and after that she had had a back operation but she'd be going home soon.

'Can I send you some pictures? Would you like that?' I asked her. Oh yes, and she gave me her address, the one that Marcus had unearthed in Fort Lauderdale.

After forty-five exhilarating and exhausting minutes, we hung up. 'It's so much to take in!' she exclaimed.

184

'It is, but we have time now.'

'Yes!' she said emphatically.

The next day I pounced on the phone at 9 a.m. Florida-time. Her voice was slightly more circumspect when she picked up the phone, but brightened when she heard mine, 'it's you!'

'I won't pester you, I promise, but I don't know your birthday. It seemed like something I should know, after all, you know mine.'

'September 28, exactly six months before or after yours! You were conceived at 328 East 90th Street!' It blasted out of her, she had waited to say these words for a long time, these coincidences that connected us that she had wanted to share for almost fifty years. I only understood the significance of 'three twenty-eight' when Mira said it, instead of reading it in the newspaper articles. It's my birthday.

From there, we established a routine. I would propose a time for my next call and then ask, is that okay with you? We both needed a little time between calls to digest the intense emotions and volume of information. From the first phone call onwards, she recognised my voice. 'Hello Mama Mira!' I would start, 'hello Daughter Donna!' she would finish in our own call and response. We hung up when she got a frog in her throat – 'that damn frog is here again!' because she sadly wasn't used to talking so much.

The package of photos of me at different ages and some of Dexter and Simon and the cat was disappointingly returned to me some months later, stamped with 'unknown at this address'. 'Are you still at the rehab center?' I asked. 'Yeah, maybe you should send them here for now.'

I fell hard for my mother, like a first love. I felt the height-ened perception of reality, infused with euphoria. We were fated to meet, we were meant for each other and we'd known each other our whole lives and would for the rest of time and we were just filling in all the colours and detailing. We marvelled at the amazing coincidences that were both kismet but also missed chances. I replayed our conversations over and over in my mind. My heart thumped between the first ring of the phone and when she picked up. She was all I talked about. My ear reddened from the receiver pressed hard against my head so I could catch every nuance of emotion in her voice. I savoured each nugget of information, any similarity to myself was imbued with deep significance.

'Did you have any other children?' I asked early on.

'Oh no, just you.'

Alvin was the love of her life but after they lost track of each other – I assumed that was after she went home and gave me up and he went to jail – she had met another man, Bruce, while working at the bank. It was an 'important' relationship but nothing like what she had with Alvin – it's not every man you fake your own death for, after all.

She had moved to Florida to be with Bruce and she liked living by the water and the boats in Fort Lauderdale. While she was home on a visit to her mother Bruce had suddenly died, but she stayed on in Florida because by that time his relatives felt like family to her.

We talked about the foods we loved, books we'd read. She couldn't really read any more as her eyesight was quite poor. It wasn't the macular degeneration as she had reported to Louise Wise Services in 1993, just normal age-related deterioration. Did she like books on tape? I asked. 'I don't really know,' she answered. I vowed to send her some.

As well as craving mothering from Mira, I wanted to reciprocate by caring for her as a daughter would, to cook for her and read her favourite books to her. I baked her a batch of oatmeal, chocolate-chip cookies and sent them in the mail.

They must have been reduced to stale crumbs after the week they took to reach her but she claimed they were delicious. 'I can tell they were baked with love.'

I confided to her that I was close with my mother before she died. 'I was close with my mother, too,' Mira said. Mira had grown up speaking Russian at home and her mother was a great cook. Ruth was a horrible cook, but on the plus side she taught me to speak French. This parallel closeness helped start to paper over the gaping holes left by our early parting and allowed us to talk tangentially about our mother-dautghter relationships.

She talked mostly of her mother, but she still had a sister who lived in North Carolina.

'Where?' I interrupted.

'The Research Triangle area.'

'My dad lives in Chapel Hill! We'll be there at Christmas!'

Another coincidence! Her sister and nephew lived there and her niece, a research biologist of some kind, also lived and worked in the area. The niece was divorced with two children. 'We're not too close,' she said. She'd also drifted away from Bruce's family.

She admitted that she had had her doubts about meeting me when she first received the letter from her lawyer about the match. She hemmed and hawed, unsure she wanted to open up that giant can of worms. To what end? I understood. For me it was a lot less ambiguous once Ruth had died. For Mira, it opened the door not just to the daughter she had given up, but other long-buried memories.

'I had just decided that I had to meet you, and then lo and behold you called.'

Woven through her stories, there was the advertised intelligence and wit, but I also sensed that Mira was guarded and wary. She was cagey about the details of her hospital stay and her future whereabouts, hesitant to make any specific plans. I couldn't decide whether that was a true impression or not, whether or not it was entirely normal to be circumspect in this extraordinary situation or whether she was naturally reticent. I couldn't know if I was reading too much into her reserve. The last time we were together, I was one week old and she was headed to prison. We had nothing to go by.

For my part, however, I recognised the impetuous enthusiasm within me, and I took heart. My joyful persistence had eventually eroded Simon's English reserve after all. I would melt Mira's heart given time. Our phone calls felt like a prelude, a rehearsal for when we would meet one another in person and start our relationship in earnest. Like Simon and me during our long-distance dance at the beginning of our relationship when he lived in London and I was in New York, the phone calls and letters marked the time, stand-ins for the real thing when we were together.

I shied away from asking about the adoption. I had read of her joy in conceiving me and her anguish at letting me go. And as ever, I was eager to please and I didn't dare risk offending or upsetting her.

'Over the years, as I saw more single mothers I wondered if I should have done that,' she offered one night.

'I think that would have been really hard,' I told her softly.

'Maybe I should have tried.'

'There's no stigma anymore, but, it's still really hard,' I said. 'I don't think I could do it.' I couldn't imagine facing all the challenges of the last seven years alone.

Days after I had first called Mira, her co-worker at the Police Academy, Terry, wrote to me. It was Terry who provided Brenda with Mira's number; she and Mira had been good friends. 'I used to visit her in the nursing home but about a year ago she just seemed to not want company anymore and I stopped going.' When I told her who I was, she became a bit more forthcoming but declined to tell me why or for how long Mira had been in what Terry referred to as, the nursing home.

Mira had confided in her, over the course of their chats at work, that she had a daughter who she had given up for adoption. 'Mira and I had our best conversations in the ladies' room at work (strange place but it was private and that was when we got to talk).' Terry was very glad that Mira and I were in touch. Her own sister had given a child up for adoption. Later in life, when she eventually found her again, the daughter wasn't ready for reunion and by the time she was, Terry's sister had already passed away. 'Her daughter said she thought she had more time.'

I asked Terry to visit Mira if she could. If finding Mira had been seismic in my life, I couldn't fathom the effect on Mira, who, although she lived with the knowledge of me, had had no prior warning of my arrival beyond the lawyer's letter that she had parked on the back burner. I worried about her processing it all by herself. I was glad when Terry promised to visit Mira over the Christmas holiday.

On December 15, I wrote to Anne at Spence-Chapin and told her that I had found Mira and that it was going well but I wondered if she had any advice for us on how to proceed. 'I want to go gently and I really want this to work and be fulfilling for both of us,' I wrote. 'I know people sometimes start off great and then things come up: anger, neediness, intrusive expectations and contact is lost again. I do not want that to happen to Mira and me. I don't want to have intruded upon her life, only to open up painful memories and then lose touch with her.' I didn't hear back from Anne for over a month so I continued calling Mira and we kept talking.

Our Christmas trip to North Carolina that year was tightly

scheduled. It was the third year of the Ruth Freed Memorial Concert and there was by then a rigid routine of organising, rehearsing and other assorted errands associated with the concert and reception that followed. Bearing in mind that it was the primary reason we were there, it was even more bizarre that all the preparation was undertaken without once mentioning Ruth in front of Dad's omnipresent girlfriend, Sylvia. Unfortunately, there was no time to add Florida to the itinerary let alone look for Mira's sister while I was there, not that I possessed enough information to even start. It was deliciously excruciating to know that my aunt and cousins lived somewhere close by.

My brother spent New Year's Eve with the Fish family in Upper Montclair, New Jersey and Selma remembered Mira very well. She told Paul that the pair of them frequented the same bar in town. Selma always liked Mira even though she had a 'seedy boyfriend'. According to Selma, Mira was quiet and nice, an intelligent woman who was forever reading, and they always talked about books.

Throughout the spring, over long phone calls I formed a picture of her and of her life, but it was as though those phone calls and our relationship occurred on a separate spatial and temporal plane – and in a sense they did. They existed solely between the two of us, always on the phone and during my late evening hours when I could devote the time to her, and in between the routines of hospital life, the rigour of bath times and mealtimes which dictated her hours – not dissimilar to the routines of home and motherhood that I adhered to. We lived in our own audio bubble. While it was disorienting to have a mother I hadn't yet met, I was tethered to her disembodied voice, like a voice on the radio, or a wire-tap.

14

ONCE UPON A TIME IN HOLLYWOOD, FLORIDA (2012)

We were headed to the States for our family reunion and to meet Mira. I channelled all my mounting anxiety about meeting her in person into the crucial question of what to wear. It was like picking an outfit for a first date or choosing a wedding dress. Obviously, there was no dress code for this kind of occasion, but it certainly qualified as an 'occasion' and therefore, in my mind, required a dress. Trousers, jeans, or a skirt would not do. The only other garment I could have envisaged was a jumpsuit, but this was August in South Florida, it was bound to be scorching and filthy with humidity.

My meet-my-mother dress was sleeveless with a fitted, navy top and a tulip skirt belling out from a cinched waist. The skirt was white with blue and orange polka dots in rows like the beads of an abacus. It felt flattering, playful and presentable; in short, it was a dress a mother could only love.

We had trekked out to the Outer Banks of North Carolina, back to Trinity Center, the scene of Dad's 75th birthday celebration with Irmgard, seven years earlier, when I was pregnant with Dexter. It was a familiar landscape, but a wholly altered experience, for while Leah, Paul and I were all there with our families and Dad as before, gone were Ruth and Lewis. Irmgard, while still alive, was also absent: not only was she not fond of Seymour, she was even less fond of his girlfriend, Sylvia. We were assigned a different cluster of cabins. Their construction was identical to those we had stayed in before, but their location, on the opposite side of the site, was disorienting. We arrived at the beach, the pool and the dining hall from unexpected angles contributing to the off kilter feeling.

Dad was almost exclusively preoccupied with the marshalling of Sylvia; his every word was calculated to remind her who and where she was. We resentfully helped him bolster this reality, but it was tough going. We were not patient; we were not understanding. Beyond the dementia, she was wrathful, her anger an echo of Mom's of old. We learned unfortunate lessons from that irrational anger, it had trained us to deem any aberrant behaviour as an inconvenience and an imposition.

'She makes me feel so young,' Dad trumpeted whenever possible. Regardless of how he felt, he looked absolutely shattered with the effort of keeping up appearances. When it was time to leave, Sylvia was disoriented and paranoid and attempted to pack the pictures on the wall into her suitcase, but at least she hadn't wandered off this time.

I was already in a heightened state of anxious expectation, amplified by the hyper-vigilance needed to keep watch over Sylvia, a state that easily tipped over into hysteria.

We signed up for a night beach at the North Carolina

Aquarium to see the nesting sea turtles, but rain made the conditions impossible, so instead, our exuberant guide took us on an after hours tour of the aquarium. We went behind the displays to view tanks of back-up stingrays and incubating alligators and caimans. We peered into the lionfish sick bay, their ragged, chiffon-like brown-and-white fins ruffled in the open-topped tanks.

The aquarium's star attraction was the living shipwreck display, a massive tank with a replica of a sunken German U-Boat and filled with sharks, a sea turtle and a moray eel among other fish native to these waters. Leah and I lagged behind as we walked around the open rim of the shark tank, the grey forms circling below, a flimsy white plastic chain keeping us from the divers' entry point and the ladder into the tank. I was drawn to the tank's edge, entranced, dragged towards it as if pulled by a centripetal force. The slam of the door echoed over the water and Leah and I were alone with the sharks and I hadn't seen which door the rest of the party exited through. My mind flipped through my mental rolodex of emergency procedures, but there was no entry for 'locked in a shark tank'. We finally found the right door and ran down the stairs, shrieking with uncontainable, relieved laughter.

Paul had already made the journey to meet his birth mother and I would literally be following in his footsteps to meet Mira. Both our mothers, erstwhile clients of Louise Wise Services, were now residents of Broward County, Florida. Leah had taken the same steps as Paul and I had, but had so far not found her birth family, so I told Leah I'd look for her mother when I was there. If ours were there, surely Leah's should be too.

I called Mira to remind her that we were coming shortly and which day. 'Soon, Mama Mira.' 'Yes, Daughter Donna,' she replied. We were trying to create family history and traditions, to carve out something for ourselves.

Whereas Paul and Leah were excited for me, Dad was completely ambivalent. 'Good luck,' he said. It struck me as an odd thing to say, but meeting my birth mother did feel serendipitous and a bit precarious, like luck might well play a role in furthering what fate has ordained. In any event, wishing me luck was as much of a blessing to the endeavour as Dad could muster.

I hadn't been to Florida since high school and it was an assault on the senses. The taxi catapulted north in fits and starts on I-95, the traffic was intense, the driving aggressive and the lanes ill-defined. The humidity and pollution blurred the palm trees as we hurtled through Miami to Hollywood. We cruised through inland Hollywood, one long strip mall to the coast and the Hollywood Broadwalk. For our short stay, we booked into the Crown Plaza, which seemed to have a mostly Russian clientele. Our balcony faced north with views of the intercoastal waterway to the west and the ocean to the east. We splashed around in the pool and collected palm fronds and coconuts on the beach. We ate burgers at Le Tub overlooking the intercoastal.

Everything was tinged with unreality, as if I were watching a film of myself. I noticed everything and felt nothing. I was breathless, gulping to take everything in. I was floundering with stage fright in the face of meeting my mother, pre-date jittery, butterflies with a side of nausea.

I trembled with caffeine and nerves in the shower, my breath shallow.

'Should I wear the plain dangly earrings or the daisy dangly ones?' I asked Simon.

'I don't think it matters, she's not going to love you any

less,' he said and, drawing me to him, kissed me on the top of my head.

I opted for the plain dangly ones, you never know.

I picked up the phone with shaking hands. 'Good morning, Mama Mira,' I said softly. 'Today's the day, are you ready?'

'I don't know. I feel like I was always ready, but I'm nervous.'

'Me too. The computer says it should take about fifteen minutes. Should I leave here in about fifteen minutes?'

'Make it half an hour.'

I bristled, primed for rejection. 'This is much bigger for her than it is for you,' Simon reminded me.

So I sat on the bed and watched Spongebob with Dexter. Spongebob tried in vain to teach Patrick how to play hide-and-seek. Mira, on the other hand, seemed to have mastered the game.

The cab made its torturous stop-start way past the endless single-storey stores, hitting every possible red light. We finally pulled up under the awning of a boxy, ochre-coloured, two-storey building located next to the much larger Memorial Regional Hospital. I signed the guestbook at the reception desk. 'You wanna go back or wait here for someone to bring you back?'

'I'll wait here, if that's okay.'

The minutes stretched by and just as I jumped up to go and find the room myself, a nurse named Tanya arrived.

'Oh my God! You're her daughter. You look like her,' she exclaimed. Mira must be excited if she told someone.

'I'm meeting her for the first time.'

'I know,' she said. 'I remember when my daughter met her half-sister for the first time, she was so excited, she said they had the same ears.'

She walked in front of me down the semi-dark,

low-ceilinged hallway painted a dirty pink. The doors to the rooms that lined the hallway were open to reveal patients in bed, watching TV, visiting with family or calling for the nurses. I kept my eyes on the nurse's back. The smell of stewed food and chemical disinfectant didn't fully mask the more putrid odours. Tanya stopped and looked back at me at the door of Room 116, just past the nurse's station. I took a breath and then nodded my readiness. The room was divided into two by curtains. Tanya pulled back the curtain closest to the door.

'Mira, your daughter's here,' she sang out.

There was a chair at the end of the bed by the door, next to the small television sat on a chest of drawers. There was a folded-up wheelchair tucked in the corner.

Her forehead was smooth, her white hair fluffed around her face, which was dominated by her thick glasses. Her hazel grey eyes appeared small because of the prescription. She was sitting up but looked strapped in.

'Hello, Donna!' she held her arms out to me.

She was hugging me and I was hugging her and we were both crying. I was in my mother's arms at last.

When we pulled away, I went to sit down but the only chair was so far away and even though I had so many questions for her, it felt too much like an interrogation, too confrontational, to sit facing her on the bed. I turned and lay down next to her. We leant into each other, our hands reaching out.

'We have the same thumbs!'

We sat shoulder to shoulder, holding out our thumbs and grinning. Her hands were soft and bony with knobbly knuckles. We held hands while we talked, her hands moving over mine, feeling out their shape, running over each finger.

'Oh, the wonderment of it all,' she said, with a squeeze.

She told me about her life in New York before she met Alvin. She had two close friends, Arle Gaines and Pat Dowd. 'I would make my famous chilli and we'd drink a lot of red wine,' Mira said with a twinkle. Now that really could be a mirror of my own New York existence!

She paused to say, 'I love your hair.'

'So if it isn't you and it wasn't Alvin, who had the curly hair?'

'I guess it's just you.'

She had a boyfriend before Alvin but she broke it off because he was an alcoholic and he had a 'running party in his pants.' I looked at her blankly.

'A running party?'

'He slept around,' she said and we laughed.

She confided that she had twice gone to Puerto Rico, to undergo two terminations before she was pregnant with me. 'It was awful, everyone else was packed up to go on vacation and I was there to do that.' I looked it up later and before the 1973 Supreme Court Roe v Wade decision, women could obtain legal abortions in Puerto Rico.

I asked her to tell me about Alvin. 'Well, he referred to himself as Thane John Stewart Balancourt and claimed he was a Thane of Brodie.' The Thanes of Brodie were the earliest known chiefs of the Scottish Brodie Clan. This particular Thane of Brodie had a Bassett Hound named Max.

'You said he was a writer?' I asked Mira.

'He wrote poetry. It wasn't very good,' she conceded, 'but he enjoyed writing it. He wrote all the time.'

'Why Spain? Where?'

'Alvin said he wanted to go to Spain,' she shrugged.

'If he had collected the money, do you think you would have gone?'

'That's what he said.' She still believed in him after all

these years even though she already knew everything there was to know.

I asked about Thomas Martin and the 'third man' who picked her up in a motorboat. 'Some friend of Alvin's' is all she said, and I didn't know if she was referring to Thomas Martin or the motorboat man, but I could tell she wasn't interested in saying more. Whether it was all so long ago or my questions felt like the same intrusive nosiness she'd always encountered I couldn't work out.

She changed the subject, 'I liked Alvin's wife, Louise, she was a nice woman.' I wondered what circumstances had come to pass for her to speak warmly of Alvin's wife and if the feeling has been mutual. She didn't say but she added that she liked his kids too. She mentioned three boys and a girl. The newspaper reports didn't mention any daughters, only four boys. That mystery would take another few years to resolve.

'I found so many articles, what was that like, all the publicity?'

'It was so awful, the whole thing. The worst was when the *Daily News* published their 'Justice Story' that dredged the whole thing back up again.'

'Did you really buy Alvin a Jaguar?'

'I wish, I have no idea where they got that Jaguar business. We had no money, so we just walked and walked. We walked from one end of Manhattan to the other.' She saw a poet and a dreamer where others saw a fantasist and a schemer. And while we read the lurid reports – myself included – and rubber-necked her calamitous bus wreck, her heart broke all over again.

I went to the guest bathrooms by the front door. There was excrement smeared on the floor of the first stall, so I used the other one. The dingy hallway, despite being on the ground floor, felt like a basement. I tried not to take in the shabby surroundings and hoped the smell didn't seep into my dress.

Back in her room, I told Mira about staying in Miami Beach in the early 1980s when the Art Deco hotels were crumbling and all the signs were in French to cater for the French Canadian 'snow birds' who spent their winters there. That was before her time in Florida. Her boyfriend, Bruce, had an apartment near Hendricks Isle, a network of waterways and canals that was a haven for bootleggers during the Prohibition era.

'I liked all the boats. We used to hang out down there with the liver boards.'

'Liver boards?' I queried.

'Live-aboards, people who live on their boats,' she explained, laughing at me. I liked her for that, it meant she was comfortable, not scared of offending me.

I was already under the impression that Mira, despite her protestations that she'd be home soon, had been at Hollywood Hills for years and wasn't going anywhere; she was there for the long-haul. When I had told her over the phone that I bought a new dress to wear to meet her, she said 'I'll be wearing a gown ... a hospital gown. I'm not sure I have any clothes here.'

'Will they help put you in a chair when I come?'

'They could, but it would mean using the hoist,' was her non-committal reply.

The dim hallway that I had walked down, where the light from the windows didn't quite penetrate, was the rehab part of the facility where people recovering from operations recuperated before going home. The hallway that started at the nurse's station, Mira's hallway, was in the nursing home side of the building. I trained my focus on Mira and what was important in this moment. This was our moment to be there together, side by side, with the same thumbs.

She explained that after her back operation, she was learning to walk again. She had a physical therapist who had encouraged her walking with a hand at her elbow. That therapist was replaced with a new person who put a belt around Mira's waist to urge her forward. 'It made me feel like a donkey, I hated it. After that,' she said, 'I got lazy.' She shifts her thin legs beneath the blanket and while there was the physical potential to leave this bed, there didn't seem to be the will.

Mira's roommate in Bed B, by the window, sometimes moaned but she could no longer speak. 'She's been here a long time, as long as I can remember. Her family comes to visit every day, I'm jealous of that.'

We had arranged for Simon and Dexter to arrive at lunch-time along with Mira's friend and co-worker Terry, who was bringing pepperoni and mushroom pizza, something Mira really missed. Terry wanted to witness our reunion and it would hopefully take some of the pressure off Mira to have a friend there.

I heard the quick slap of Dexter's sandalled feet in the hallway just before his arrival. 'I think we're getting visitors,' I told Mira. 'Simon and Dexter are here.'

Just as her nervous glance darted towards the door, the curtain flew open and the blur of seven-year-old Dexter was at her side, his face pushing up into hers, 'Grandma!' he shouted and threw his arms around her neck. Mira tipped her head back and laughed, clasping him to her chest.

Dexter got right down to business and without further ado, whipped out his pack of cards and performed his best, and only, magic trick. Mira was mystified, astonished and congratulatory in all the right places and with that, she had elevated herself to the role of grandmother, her first task completed with aplomb.

Terry arrived with the pizza and there was the happy hubbub of meetings and greetings. Terry helped Mira eat her pizza, 'It's so good,' she said, 'I've missed this.' It worked, Mira was pleased to see Terry and have someone in her corner and Terry was happy to have facilitated the reunion and seemed to sense that we were genuine and not there to take advantage of Mira in any way. I was relieved that Simon and Dexter seemed to like her, to see what I see in her.

After lunch, Terry left us to carry on our visit and I took Dexter to the toilet. This time the clean stall was occupied so we had to use the dirty one. 'What's that?' Dexter recoiled from the shit on the floor. 'Just don't step in it,' I answered.

I didn't want him to notice. I didn't want him to not like Mira because she was in this shit-hole. It was hard to accept that my mother was in this grim place for all sorts of reasons, but I would deal with that later. I didn't want anything to tarnish our reunion day with Mira.

Back in Room 116 – Bed A, we presented Mira with our gifts. Dexter handed over a red London bus so she could picture us on the top deck in the front seats. 'We always sit there,' Dexter told her, nodding seriously. Simon gave her a CD player and CDs of *To Kill a Mockingbird* and I presented her with two heart cockle shells. 'One for each of us,' I told her. They were bleached white and looked like two hearts back-to-back or two sets of furled wings fused together. We each took one and ran our identical thumbs over their chalky ridges.

The conversation was warm and light. Simon mentioned being continually pursued by mosquitoes from North Carolina to Florida. 'They're vicious down here,' Mira said, 'they come after you with knives and forks.'

Other than the occasional doctor or hospital administrator, the rehab centre was a largely female domain. Mira found being bathed by the rare male nurse or attendant deeply discomforting, but she peered at Simon with avid interest. She was flirtatious and forward with him, looking at him directly. At the end of the afternoon, when her roommate's daughter arrived to feed her mother dinner, Mira was eager for Simon's goodbye kiss.

Simon and Dexter went to wait for the taxi, leaving me to say my goodbyes to Mira in semi-private. I crouched next to her, leaning over to hug her. I took in her musty hair. She looked away from me and then down. I thought she was turning away from me, but she was looking back in time.

'I remember holding you,' she said, her hands turned up as if I were still in her arms. 'I remember holding you and unwrapping you and how scared I was. And here we are now.'

She sounds just as scared and wondrous now as she must have then. I am both that babe in her arms and the one holding her and I am so grateful I am here to hear these words.

And then I unglue myself from Mira and say goodbye.

We breakfasted on bagels and coffee with her the following morning. We missed our flight out and because it was Labor Day, spent endless hours traipsing from gate to gate through Miami airport with an increasingly anxious Dexter trying to fly standby. I didn't tell Mira about that until we were safely back in London, I did not want this visit that had solidified our connection to be tainted by failure in any way.

Mira's stories made me want to know more about Alvin Brodie, or Thane John Stewart Ballancourt, as he preferred.

Brutus Cain and John Scott were also aliases he employed according to one of the *Daily News* articles from the time of their arrests.

In his 1991 'Justice Story' follow up that so upset Mira, Joseph McNamara used a heavy hand to paint a dim portrait of Alvin:

'A skinny, goateed fellow clung in fright to the side of the sturdy capsized craft, its outboard stilled. A clean-shaven man dove deep into the blue waters under a cloudless sky.

"What happened?" asked one of the fishermen, off-duty Detective Barth Giacobello, as he hauled the small, bearded man from the water . . .

His beard dripping into a puddle the rescued man explained that he – Alvin Brodie – could not swim, while his pal was a good swimmer . . .

In dry clothes and warmed by coffee, Brodie told cops about the ill-fated outing on Pelham Bay . . .

As Brodie told it, the time on the briny had been pleas-ant, a little fishing, mostly cruising under the hot sun. Mira fell asleep, he told cops, and he thought it would be fun to awaken her with a playful spray of water.

So Brodie zig-zagged the boat in hopes of a light spray, he said. Instead, the craft took on water rapidly at the stern and began to overturn.

"My God, I panicked," Brodie said, trembling, his eyes moist. "I jumped over the side." Which could have served nothing, since he could not swim.

When the Lindenmaiers were questioned by lawmen in their Upper Montclair, N.J. home . . . her father said . . . "Who's this Brodie? I never heard her talk of him."

Who indeed? Detective Edward Dermody, who now took charge of the case, learned that Mira had met Brodie in a taproom, that he lived with his wife, Louise, and four children, aged two to fourteen.'

An even later article in 2019 in the *New York Post* unearthed a quote from Louise from their archives:

'Alvin's wife, who read of his exploits in the newspaper, told *The Post* she was "terribly nervous and upset about the whole thing" but that she didn't plan to leave her husband. Her hair in rollers as she looked after her boys at the "shabbily furnished" flat, Louise was asked if [sic] she her marriage was a happy one.

She replied: "How many happy marriages are there?"'

Alvin was the only one of the three defendants in the case to be jailed. Anne's background report cited 'other fraud charges' for denying bail. Copies of the original Prisoner's Criminal Records from 13 December, 1966, show that Thomas Martin had no prior arrests and was that day charged with Attempted Grand Larceny, Conspiracy and Obstruction of Justice. Miriam Lindenmaier 'AKA Mira Lindenmaier' also had no priors and was charged only with Attempted Grand Larceny. Alvin's record shows the same charges as Martin and only one prior charge. He had been arrested almost exactly two years earlier on 11 December 1964 on a charge of Attempted Grand Larceny. The arresting officer was detailed as Meenan of the 20th Squad on the Upper West Side of Manhattan. This would have been a year into his three-year relationship with Mira and presumably the reason his sentence was not suspended, although the felony charge was later dropped.

The New York City Municipal Archives hold records of the original case, Indictment 48/67, in a file of materials relating to an appeal made by Alvin against his conviction. Unfortunately, if there are any transcripts of the wire-taps or original recordings, they remain restricted and unavailable.

Alvin's appeal was based on a writ of coram nobis, which is a request to reopen an already decided case because the verdict that was reached hinged upon a mistake, a mistake that could now be rectified. In this instance, the case had already been decided because all of the defendants pleaded guilty to the charges. However, ignoring that inconvenient detail, Alvin pressed ahead, claiming that the decision was based solely upon the evidence of the wire-tap and that the wire-tap was illegal. If the wire-tap constituted an illegal search, as was found to be the case in Berger vs New York, and thus a violation of his constitutional rights, then the wire-tap evidence and all the evidence that was gathered because of it was also illegal and therefore inadmissible. Ergo, case capsized and his conviction should be overturned.

His handwritten appeal was most likely written in his cell at Riker's Island. His handwriting leans to the right, driving forward with urgency and confidence. As he seemed to be acting as a lawyer on his own behalf, he referred to himself in the third person as 'the defendant.'

The opening paragraph reads:

'The defendant makes motions to the court for dismissal of his conviction and indictment in the above case in the form of a Corum Novice Motions.'

This was taken to mean coram nobis. He continues:

'The defendant in making this request bases his argument on the recently publicized cases of Berger vs New York, and also on the more recent case of the three men who were awaiting trial in Brooklyn for the murder of an informer.

It has been stated, and the court records will bare [sic] me out, by the District Attorney, Bertram Roberts, that, (and I quote), had it not been for wiretap evidence, we would never have been able to indict the defendant on this charge. (end of quote); now it is the defendants contention that, since all other admissions and evidence obtained by the District Attorney was brought on by, whether directly, or indirectly, as a result of this wiretap evidence. Thus none of the evidence is valid.'

He argued that if wire-tap evidence was considered illegal in these other cases, so should it apply to his. His letter was received by the Supreme Court Clerk's Office of Bronx County on 20 September 1967.

In Berger vs New York, the wire-tap evidence gathered by New York State was deemed inadmissible due to insufficient probable cause and the bribery conviction of a state official was overturned. The wire-tap was seen as a violation of the fourth Amendment of the Constitution of the United States of America, which protects citizens from unreasonable searches and seizures and requires probable cause. The police cannot just go on a fishing expedition because they think you're a bad apple, regardless of what they might find, whether it be bribery, murder or insurance fraud.

Alvin's request was swiftly shot down. Because he, standing with Thomas Martin and Mira and her parents, pleaded guilty to the charges which were brought with evidence gained initially by the wire-tap and did not dispute that evidence at the time of pleading, Alvin was not allowed to then demand an investigation into whether there was sufficient probable cause to grant the all-important wire-tap in the first place. That decision would remain unchallenged, although the timing of the beneficiary change and the supposed death was rather damning, and then there was the not inconsequential matter of Mira's voice on the wire-tap.

Alvin's relentless, feral energy crafted his words, evidence of his wily arrogance. There was itch and fight in him that alchemized into his brazen chutzpah. His agile mind was always on the lookout for the next angle, a way out. Alvin, Thane of Brodie was owed and he was not going down without a fight. I could see the appeal.

15

ASPECIAL PLACE IN HELL
(2012–2017)

I was flattened in the wake of meeting Mira. In the run up to our reunion, I had been skipping above the surface of my life, forging ahead on the froth of events. Afterwards I felt like I'd fallen down a well and was scrabbling to regain purchase; it was a struggle to just keep pace with life.

Part of this lassitude was post-event deflation, the anti-climactic exhaustion that seeps in after a sustained effort to reach one moment. After our forty-four-year-long separation, there had been over a year's build up leading to our reunion in Room 116, Bed A which was both wedding and honeymoon rolled into one and over in two days. In that year of yearning anticipation, I had snatched at details as I galloped by and now I had time to reflect and sift through the many years-worth of information and stored up emotions.

Simon had warned me against investing too much in my meeting with Mira but how could I not? She wasn't just some woman, a random acquaintance, she was my mother, and even in this short time, we had come to care deeply about each other. But in making our connection a reality instead of a dream, by restarting the clock, I could see just how much time had gone irrevocably by. In attempting to bridge it, the vastness of the gap between us was made starkly apparent.

'And here we are,' she had said. Mira and I had travelled far and wide in the decades between when she last held me in New York Hospital and when I held her in Hollywood Rehab Center.

It was with deep regret that I also had to acknowledge my sad disappointment that while Mira was my biological parent, she was not my mother. My heart had assigned that role to one woman. 'You only have one mother,' as Lew said. And now, the mourning for Ruth that I bypassed through my all-consuming search for Mira, was there waiting for me, just where I had left it.

I think Mira also mourned the lost time that robbed her of being a mother and knowing her daughter. I couldn't be the same kind of daughter that she had been to Braina. I was that daughter to Ruth. I sensed that she too expected her life to transform upon my return, that I would rescue her in some way. I was supposed to be the prodigal daughter and redemptive white knight in one, and it was a heavy burden to shoulder.

But this feeling of deflation and depression; I thought this too shall pass. It was a phrase of Mira's mother's, my grand-mother's, that Mira repeated to me. It was a true family heirloom in that it was passed from mother to daughter through shared time, conversation and habitual repetition. Mira and I began, slowly but surely, to accrue our own mem-ories through more phone calls and regular if not frequent visits.

But as ever, life did not stand still to afford me the time

to ponder and absorb. No sooner were we back from Florida than Simon's mother suffered a stroke. That same weekend we put in an offer on our first home. As soon as we closed on the house, I started driving lessons, learning to drive on the wrong side of the car, on the wrong side of the road and with a manual transmission, or 'stick' as Mira and I would say.

I kept Mira updated on all our comings and goings. She always asked after Dexter and the cat, wanting to keep track and be included. I added Florida to my bi-annual trips to the States and fantasised about renting an apartment for a few weeks, taking Mira out to the beach, pressing her blanched feet in the warm sand while watching the sunset.

I tried not to think about the last time she'd looked out of a window. I felt powerless and ashamed when I thought about her circumstances but I didn't know what to do about it. I didn't know enough about the situation, and frankly, I didn't know Mira. I couldn't waltz back in after forty four years and start dictating.

I remembered reading adopted novelist Amy M. Homes' *New Yorker* article about her birth parents. After only two meetings with her birth mother, she had occasion to go through her mother's jeans pockets where she found cash wadded and stuffed into the pockets in the exact same way she did. The arrangement of her pockets, a seeming biological marker, not a matter of choice. I did not witness Mira move through the world so I only had our thumbs to go by. Would I lie supine in a bed the same way she did? Mira lay there prone and defeated, while Ruth sat on her bed like she was sitting at a desk, it was both a place of refuge as well as the seat of her power. Which one was my mirror?

I deferred my calls to Mira for different reasons and excuses than I used to delay calling my parents. If my mother was my witness, I could retard the reality of an event by not telling her. As soon as it was reported, it became real. I would be forced to call when the procrastination infected my dreams with dental nightmares. My teeth would fall out at the slightest touch. I would pull huge, mottled, red dinosaur-sized teeth unendingly out of my mouth or it would fill with mud and putty that would set like concrete while I scraped and scooped it out. Waking with my heart pounding, I would make the connection and finally make that phone call.

With Mira, the fact that I had to face was that if I didn't pick up the phone, it would never ring. There was an arc of procrastination tied to the frequency of my phone calls. Around the two-week mark following a call, my conscience gave a nudge to call Mira. From this initial prod to the actual call might take a day but more often than not, weeks. There was a reluctance, an anticipatory dread born out of resentment at the obligation; the tension grew with the delay. In order to speed up the process, I would tell Simon, 'I need to call Mira.'

When days passed, he followed up, 'Have you called Mira?'

'Not yet, but I will.' When I eventually picked up the phone, we chatted and laughed and I was always smiling when I hung up, but sometimes it took a huge effort to make the call.

One afternoon I phoned and oddly, she didn't answer. The only time she left the room was when they wheeled her into the hallway to mop. I tried again later and the next day. I called the nurse's station. 'The phone fell on the floor; you can try her again now.' When I asked her how long it had been on the floor, she said she didn't know.

She passed each day in much the same way and even when something out of the ordinary occurred, she didn't always think to tell me. When I sent her anything, I always had to ask. 'Did you get the flowers we sent?' The pictures of Dexter and the Pox? The chocolates?

She didn't tell me her roommate passed away, but the bed was empty on my next visit. 'Will you move to the other side by the window?' I asked her. 'No, I like to know what's going on out there,' she tilted her head towards the hallway.

'I knew you would pass,' she told me when I aced the theory test and she bellowed her congratulations when I passed the driving test at my third attempt. 'I only passed because we just had a hurricane and a bunch of trees were down so we had to go on a shorter route.'

'Who cares,' she said. 'You passed! I knew you could do it.'

Once I apologised for how long it had been between calls and visits. 'That's okay,' she said. 'When I miss you, I just look at my thumbs.'

On another call, she announced out of the blue, 'I've decided to change my will. I'm going to make you the beneficiary instead of my sister.'

'Wow, I said, that's huge.'

It was lovely to hear her say these things. They resounded with maternal pride and the last in particular felt like a gift, a vote of confidence. She was offering what she could of herself. I didn't believe she'd do it, especially because I wondered how she would explain it to her sister without telling her sister about me, but that wasn't the point.

Visits to Florida were more rewarding but difficult to fit in between school schedules and other demands. There was one busy but not entirely atypical week in June of 2017 during which Simon's lovely mother, Nancy, died, then her half-brother died and I mistook the gas pedal for the brake and smashed the car into the wall ten feet away, denting the wall and deploying the air-bags, which left me me dazed and bruised. Dexter was accepted at a new school and the induction day was scheduled for the same day as Nancy's funeral.

I usually had Dexter in tow so visits to Mira could be tricky to navigate. We stayed at the beach so we could swim or bike up and down the Broadwalk before getting some food to take to her. Before I learned to drive, we had to call and wait for cabs. At the rehab centre, we crowded into her half room where the TV was always on. 'Can I turn this off?' I once asked. 'No,' Mira said, 'I like it on.' At least the TV helped occupy Dexter while we talked.

My nephew, who was witness to his own father's reunion with his birth mother, joined Dexter and me on one of our visits. 'This is so cool,' he said, looking at the three generations, just as I had marvelled at him with his parents and grandmother.

Mira was more talkative and open about herself when I was there in person. Because her eyes were poor and her hands quite weak, I helped her eat. We were negotiating an awkward shrimp burrito and she was chewing on the napkin instead of the tortilla. 'Hey Dexter, it's true. You are part mountain goat, you get it from your grandmother.' We all laughed. Then she let slip, 'my mother was so mad when she found out I was still seeing Alvin.'

'Wait, what? You were seeing Alvin after he came out of jail?'

'Yeah, my mother couldn't believe it, she was so mad when she found out.' I wondered what lured her back. Did she feel guilty that it was her voice that drew the cops to their doors? It was her fault that there they were back in the same old grooves instead of living it up in sunny Spain. If I asked her anything as direct as that, though, she clammed up or just said, 'I don't know.'

Most pseudocides – people who fake their own deaths – are

men looking to escape money troubles. It almost never works, but the allure of disappearing and starting over, debt-free and with a big pot of money to boot, remains a hardy perennial. Elizabeth Greenwood's book *Playing Dead: A Journey Through the World of Death Fraud* explores the subject extensively.

The number one reason for death fraud is money. Number two is violence – getting away from your organised crime associates from whom you have stolen money, say, or in the instance of one of the few female fakers, a woman who, after a brutal beating by her boyfriend, pretended to be dead convincingly enough for him to call an ambulance. She revealed her desperate hoax only once she was far enough away from his fists. Reason number three is love.

Methods obviously vary but drowning is an obvious and popular choice because it solves the first and most immediate problem for a convincing pseudocide, the lack of a body, with the added boon that it affords you precious time to make your escape. But, as Mira, Alvin and Thomas found to their cost, the lack of a body can also be a dead giveaway.

Natural disasters – earthquakes, landslides and the like – also provide a plausible explanation for the lack of a body. When two planes crashed into the World Trade Center's towers on September 11 2001, there were numerous fraudulent claims. These were both expected and all eventually exposed by the investigators.

An unrecognisable corpse is also good but poses the messy and complicated challenge of obtaining a dead body. Accidents are often staged in a different country from the one the insurance claim is being made in the hopes that the insurance company won't bother sending skip tracers – the bounty hunters of the insurance world – to find you very much alive when presumed dead.

The only success story that Greenwood encountered was

that of former school teacher and prison officer, John Darwin, the 'canoe man' as he is best known. He went to sea in his kayak and didn't report for his shift at the prison and was later presumed drowned at sea.

Mira fell into the final category for pseudocides: love, a love so blinding that it outweighed the inevitable heartbreak her loss would cause her parents. And Alvin, supposedly, did what he did for a love so eclipsing that he claimed he was prepared to abandon his wife and four children and escape with Mira to Spain to raise me in Mediterranean splendour.

Faking your own death remains, however, a perilous affair and if you're undertaking it for the purposes of collecting an insurance pay out, your plan relies entirely on at least one other person you trust to turn the money over to you. Alvin must have trusted that Mira would play her part and stay hidden and that Thomas Martin could be relied upon to keep his mouth shut.

One of the qualities that all the male pseudocides seemed to share was hubris. It was the fatal flaw that ensured the arrogant braggart's inevitable downfall. Greenwood surmised that not being able to boast about getting away with it was one of the reasons that John Darwin voluntarily turned himself in. He and his wife had just achieved a new fantasy life in Panama, riding horses on their tropical ranch, when he walked into the West End Central police station in London faking amnesia.

From what I have learned of Alvin, I doubt my birth father could stay of out of the limelight for more than half an hour. He would never have been able to lie low for the kind of quiet time required to pull off this type of scheme unless he was behind bars. Perhaps for Alvin Brodie this was pseudocide-by-proxy. He could disappear over Mira's dead body; he could use her passing as the means to his own end.

As a pseudocide-by-proxy, Alvin had more control of the situation and was also the centre of attention, the dramatic clinging to the boat, the desperate rescue attempts, the crocodile tears at Mira's watery demise.

Maybe he and Mira told themselves it was a type of passive bank robbery, a victimless crime. They would get one over on the insurance companies, nobody would get hurt and they would run off to Spain. Maybe he would have given Thomas Martin some money to look after his wife and four boys. Or maybe Alvin planned to just hightail it with the money. What was Mira going to do? Who was going to believe Elizabeth Pangborn, as Mira called herself, of White Plains?

But they made all the classic mistakes. The three key ingredients for a successful death fraud are a convincing body, money and time. Before Elizabeth Greenwood contemplated faking her own death, one of the skip tracers advised her to carefully consider her answers to three key questions.

Have you recently increased the amount of your insurance? No, but Mira abruptly changed the beneficiary on her policies, which was tantamount to the same thing as bumping up a policy's pay out from a hundred thousand to a million.

You could still redeem the situation if you answered the second question correctly. Do you have enough money to wait it out? No, Alvin was flat broke and Mira, or Elizabeth Pangborn, was making 87 cents an hour.

And finally, do you have time to wait out the insurance claim, at least two years? All of thirty-nine days after Alvin was made the beneficiary of her insurance policies, Mira had disappeared in mysterious circumstances. Alvin managed to kick his heels for a whole two months before attempting to claim the money.

Daring and romantic perhaps. The plot was long on drama

and flair but woefully short on planning and preparation and it was always doomed to fail.

I tried to match the 'double indemnity girl' of that caper with the woman before me now. I was startled by her passivity; she seemed to have given up. She wouldn't ask the nurses or attendants to pick up the phone off the floor, let alone help her listen to the CDs of books we sent. I gave the nurses my phone number and email address in London. 'I know she can't call me, but would you please let me know if she needs or wants anything?'

'She can call you. All she has to do is ask,' the nurse told me.

When I relayed this to Mira, she said, 'I don't want to bother them.'

Moments like these were hard. She reminded me of Herman Melville's 'Bartleby, the Scrivener' who responded to each request with 'I would prefer not to.' There was no social precedent for this strange relationship, no cultural norm to conform to, no rules of engagement. I had to explain my sudden appearance to the nurses and explain that, yes, I'm her daughter, but I also just met her. I won't be on her forms as next of kin. You don't have to call me and you can't give me any information. But I am her daughter. This both was and was not a mother-daughter relationship. It was an approximation of a mother-daughter relationship and that was what both Mira and I drew upon, like muscle memory from our own mothers. It was burdened by similar obligations.

Sometimes her unfulfilled mothering overcame her tongue – all those maternal instincts and scolding that lay unexpressed lo these forty-four years – as one of the symptoms of late-stage motherhood. When I called her from the airport after one visit – 'We didn't miss the plane this time!' – and then accidentally hung up on her while we were boarding.

'I'm glad you called back, because there's a special place in hell for children who hang up on their mothers,' she said with heat behind the words when we landed. It doesn't seem to matter when you become a mother, but the second you do, you immediately become your own mother, spouting all those stored-up phrases recalled from when they were shouted at you.

We were lucky though, because we genuinely liked each other. Mira was a person that I might well have been friends with if I had simply run into her in my life, the consistent reports of her intelligence and humour were not exaggerations. As my sister says, I like an old lady and do have older, maternal, women friends. It's like I've been looking for something! But however unconditional, the love for family members serves an evolutionary purpose that had long past being required in our relationship. I was not dependent on Mira for my survival and she was not bound to protect me at all costs. We met as fully formed adults, but with the weight of evolution and societal norms pressing on us from all sides.

I understood why relationships often broke down after reunion; we knew both too much and too little about each other and the expectations of each other were equally mismatched. I don't think I could have sustained the effort of our connection if Ruth had been alive. I felt bound to Mira by a mix of love, guilt, gratitude and familial obligation but it wasn't drawn from the same emotional well as my feelings for Ruth.

But I also recalled how wedded I was to Dexter when I was just three months pregnant. What if I had been forced to relinquish him after they pulled him from me. What if that had been my last and only glimpse of him? How would I have gone on from there? What would have been left of me if I hadn't had that moment when Dido was singing and I looked down at Dexter at my breast, and every moment since?

If I had learned anything in the last few years, it was that life was short and unpredictable and I could lose Mira at any moment. I resolved to take what I could get and give as much of myself and my time as I possibly could.

And then it was September 13, 2017 and I was listening to Radio 4's *PM* while making dinner when Eddie Mair said, 'six people have died after a South Florida nursing home suffered a power outage during Hurricane Irma.'

'Mum,' Dexter hollered as he came barrelling into the kitchen bursting with a homework question. I silenced him with a finger to my lips before he even opened his mouth.

'Did you hear that? I hope that's not your grandmother's nursing home!' With the millions of nursing homes in the Sunshine State, it's a near statistical impossibility that it is hers.

'Is it?' he asks, anxiety widening his eyes.

'No way!'

' . . .the nursing home, in Hollywood, Florida . . .' Eddie Mair forges on. Okay, she lived in Hollywood but still, the chances are slim to none and with those odds, it was going to have to wait. I was approaching the peak of my personal evening rush hour and I had half an hour to finish making dinner, help Dexter with his homework and take him to fencing practice. It was *not* her nursing home.

Catapulted out of the rudderless farce of whatever it was I pretended to do all day, at the chime of 3 p.m. each weekday, I would pelt to the school gates to get Dexter and then whirl into action – cleaning, sorting laundry, making dinner – safe in my role and finding refuge listening to the news.

I was keenly aware that I used to be on the other side of this equation: doing my homework at the kitchen table, NPR's *All Things Considered* on the radio, while Ruth resentfully engaged in her nightly battle to throw dinner together. The metronomic ebb and flow of the family routine were both a lifeline and a chain gang for her, and my own family's needs are the same velvet marionette strings that direct my daily dance.

In the rush out of the house that night, I forgot my phone, so I drummed my fingers through the prancing and metallic clashes of the fencing session. But when we got home there was dinner and homework to finish, and then teeth brushing and story reading.

Mira! By the time I finally checked which unfortunate facility had lost both power and six lives, it was already 10 p.m . . .

'Oh no, it is hers!' The death toll had doubled; a dozen people have died in the sweltering heat inside the home. The surviving patients had all been evacuated to Memorial Regional Hospital, located just across the street.

Now this? I have left her, waiting again. Who forgets their mother in a hurricane? Lost and found and lost again! This time through negligence!

My anxiety and guilt mounted with each unanswered ring of the nursing home's phone. Acidic, nausea-induced saliva pooled in my mouth. Changing tack, I call the Broward County Sheriff's Office who in turn transferred me to the public information officer, Janet, at the hospital.

'How can I help?' she asked. Janet sounds capable, competent and in control, a human life raft.

'I'm looking for my mother, she's a resident at the Hollywood Hills Rehab Center,' I stammered.

'What's your mother's name?' Janet asked gently.

'Mira Lindenmaier, is she okay? Has she been evacuated?'

'I can see here that she was checked in and she's okay. We're doing everything we can to keep her comfortable.' I nearly dropped the phone in my relief.

'Oh, thank goodness. Can I talk to her?'

She put me on hold to go find Mira. And then I heard her muffled voice, ' ...it's your daughter from London ...'

'Hello?

'Mira, it's Donna, are you okay?'

'Yes, yes, I'm okay. It's a bit weird, but I'm okay. I'm not really sure what happened.'

'They had to evacuate Hollywood Hills, people died! It was on the news here in London!'

'People died? I wonder if it's anyone I know. They didn't tell us anything.'

She said she was in a big ward. She was a bit confused. This must have been the first time she'd been outside in years and it was in the middle of a hurricane.

I talked her through the little I knew.

'Apparently they lost power and the back-up generators didn't work so there was no air-conditioning. You weren't hot?'

'Not particularly.'

'They said it was like 109 degrees in there! How could you not have been hot?'

'I don't think it was that hot; at least I wasn't.'

'You didn't say anything when we talked two days ago.'

'I didn't really notice anything too different. They put us out in the hallway for a while, but I didn't think too much about it.'

'I'm glad I found you!'

'Me too.'

She was in good physical shape and unscathed by the scalding heat. The following day she was moved to another nursing home in Pembroke Pines where they rushed to connect me with Mira; sadly that was to be a one-time efficiency.

'How are your new digs?'

'They're okay, Pretty similar to the old place.' she sounded blasé.

'I hope they're a little better! You do realise, Mira, that this is the second time you've made international news and the second time I've tracked you down through the Broward County Police Department!' We both laughed.

'But, Mira,' I continued, 'seriously, what if there had been a bombing or something and they bumped the story from the news and I didn't know?'

When she didn't answer, I asked if her sister had been in touch. Her niece had evidently found her just before I called.

'Have you told your family yet that we're in touch?'

'No, I haven't mentioned it.'

Well, if something happened, no one would know to call me. Maybe you should say something.'

'I'll think about it,' Mira said.

Visits to Florida became harder to schedule as my father decided to play dead. The first time we were called to his deathbed, he had fallen on the kitchen floor, in the exact spot Ruth keeled over when she tried to pick up that damned fallen milk carton. He had lain there unconscious for two days, while we called and left messages and life at the assisted living facility went on unaware. It was Lisa – who took over as Dad's girlfriend Sylvia's carer after we forced Dad to retire from that role – who found him. She had stopped by to say hello. When he didn't answer the door, she peered through the window and saw him on the floor.

It was touch and go for some weeks but he, like Ruth before him, made a miraculous recovery. It was a long road back, with his hand permanently cramped into a claw but his mind fully charged. He returned to his cottage and happily puttered around for a few months until the infection that had crept in via the wound on his hand spread throughout his body.

In surgery, they discovered the true nature of a life-threatening abscess and that he was more abscess than man. 'There was so much necrotic tissue . . .' 'I've never seen a wound like it . . .' 'It's not *if* he's going to die, but *when*.' This last sentence was repeated to me three times over the next few weeks.

I took the experts at their word and as a well-versed and efficient executrix, I swiftly went about my work. I sold the Danish Modern dining room furniture, I cancelled Dad's subscriptions and donated or recycled all of his clothing.

And then he recovered.

Several months later, I was en route to visit Mira when Dad turned blue and 'it looks bad' rerouted me to North Carolina. And then on May 28, 2018, he stopped playing and died for real. We took Mom's ashes off his closet shelf, where she had been waiting for him for almost a decade and mixed them together. We spread them on a woodland walk and held one final memorial concert.

Meanwhile, the administrative chaos that was exposed by the dramatic evacuation of Hollywood Hills was evidenced in their equally shambolic paperwork. In the vacuum, the administrators at Mira's new nursing home reached out to anyone with information. In the process of helping them with what I could, I did at least glean some information regarding the state of Mira's affairs. She was a ward of the state. I furnished them with the name of her attorney, whom I had been able to identify after Mira once mentioned him in passing. This was the party who had forwarded the letter announcing our matches on the register. He was listed as having Power of Attorney.

I appealed to him when weeks passed by and Mira didn't have any of her possessions from Hollywood Hills. 'It may sound silly,' I said, 'but there is a cockle heart shell and some other mementos.'

'I still have my thumbs,' Mira said when my calls and emails produced nothing.

It took no less than three phone calls and sometimes as many as seven to get through to Mira in her new accommodation in a nearly identical building several blocks further in from the coast. There were, however, improvements to the quality of her life. She was no longer left to languish in bed, although her feet retained the same form, pointed like a ballerina's. She was bathed before breakfast and then wheeled into the Day Room and from there to lunch. Some afternoons there was a visit with the comfort dogs who lay on her, warm and soft, or church, or a host of other activities, welcome or not.

There was a brief window, before breakfast, when I could catch her in her room. If I missed that, the next best time to call was before lunch in the Day Room, but in order to do that, I had to be transferred to the nurses' station and wait until someone was available to bring her a phone. It was difficult for her to hear in the bright room between the chatter of other residents and the TV on high. She said she missed the old place. 'Is it the people you miss?'

'Yeah, they were nice.' Hollywood Hills had somehow felt like a choice, her kind of place.

Her room was a spacious replica of her old room. There was a large, working television and a roommate by the window. I kept tabs on Mira through her friend Julie who I would not have known the existence of without the havoc of the hurricane. Julie used to visit Mira's last roommate in Hollywood Hills and she and Mira had become friends; she visited Mira most weeks and kindly emailed me updates.

I was Mira's daughter but not officially recognised as her next of kin. My only sources of information were therefore Mira and Julie. The administrators got in touch with me only if they couldn't raise a response from her lawyer, who was as vague as Mira herself. One day I got an email informing me that she hadn't had her hair washed in months because there was no money in her account. After numerous fruitless exchanges (some of them the week my father died) with the lawyer who told me, I'll call, I'll let you know, I visited, I spoke with her . . . to no satisfactory conclusion, I eventually handed over cash to fill her account.

After Mira broke a leg falling out of bed, I wrote to the lawyer: 'I am writing as you are the POA and contact for Mira. I just found out that she was admitted to the hospital again last night. I found out from Julie. Would it be possible in future to let one or both of us know if she is admitted to the hospital or of any other major incidents?'

On the morning of January 4, 2020 I landed at Fort Lauderdale airport. I stopped at Einstein Bros. Bagels to get Mira's toasted sesame bagel with a schmear, Nova lox, red onion and capers. She had asked to stay in her room knowing that I was coming and it was a relief that it was just the two of us. Over the TV, we talked. I brought her a replacement heart cockle shell and a photo album filled with pictures, including the ones from the first day we met. She was eager to hear my news. In New York, the day before, I had met Alvin's son, my half-brother Frank, and that night, after I left Mira, I was going to meet Tony, Frank's older brother and Alvin's first born.

16

FAREWELL TO ALL THAT
(2020)

In the same way that Ruth's passing had made room for Mira, in the wake of Seymour's death, now fatherless, I found my thoughts turned to Alvin's children, my half-siblings. The oldest was Tony and he would have been fourteen when his, or rather *our*, father was incarcerated, and so he might very well have got wind of my existence. Indeed, if any of them had read the 'Justice Report' in 1991, they would have known they had a half-sibling somewhere in the world. That said, I was partially responsible, albeit entirely involuntarily, for Alvin's time in prison, and I couldn't be sure that any of them would want to meet me. However, as I knew, the pull of curiosity is strong and I hoped they might see that we were all sort of in the same boat; as children, we had had no say whatsoever in what our parents got up to. We should not be judged by the sins of our shared father.

Since 2012, I had worked as a presenter on my friend Josephine's weekly radio show and then podcast, *Radio*

Gorgeous and I thought this reunion story would make for a brilliant feature. I sounded out Mira on the subject and she felt 'fine' about me looking for my half-siblings. Did she want me to let her know what I found? 'Oh yes,' she said. 'Would you let me record you for the podcast?' I asked. It was a hard 'no'.

On the morning of October 7, 2019 I stopped by Ess-a-Bagel to stock up on proper bagels before my flight home that evening. I was on my way to meet Isabel Vincent whom I had interviewed for *Radio Gorgeous* in London when she was promoting her beautiful memoir, *Dinner with Edward.* I was in the midst of writing a proposal for the podcast and felt it could easily be turned into a book as well. So, while I was looking forward to reconnecting with Isabel, I also hoped she might advise me on finding a publisher.

We met at her Rockefeller Center office in the News Corp. Building because when she isn't researching and writing books, she is an investigative reporter for the Sunday edition of the *New York Post,* an important fact that I did know but the implications of which I hadn't fully appreciated. Over coffee, I told Isabel my adoption story, the story of Alvin and Mira, the failed death fraud and my plans to find my half siblings.

'What an incredible story, Donna, do you mind if I take notes?'

By the time I landed back in London the following morning, Isabel had already emailed me the names, addresses and phone numbers of two men she suspected might be my half-brothers. 'I'm not reaching out to anyone,' she reassured me. Fears of my story being hijacked raised my hackles, but it meant a short-cut to finding my brothers. The next sentence, however, set alarm bells clamouring.

'We are very interested in doing a story.' I recoiled in horror.

This was not a good idea. I hadn't yet found or met my brothers and I didn't know if their mother, Louise, was still alive. If she was, I imagined they would be fiercely protective of her and take a dim view of publicly re-opening old family wounds. I didn't think republishing this story in the *New York Post* with its Sunday circulation of 913K would improve my chances of fostering our relationship. I most certainly could not hold a microphone under their chins after dragging their name through the mud once again and entirely for my own reasons and benefit. I felt foolish for having so blithely trotted out this story without thinking through the consequences.

Isabel followed up this email with articles from the *Post*'s archives. They had in their possession the bones of this story and could publish without my approval so I agreed but begged for a grace period. 'Isabel, please find out if Louise is alive or not!' She looked but couldn't find anything conclusive. She told me that she would use the parents' names in the story but withhold the children's. She promised to talk to her editors about holding off for a few weeks. 'This is a story that no one had heard of until a week and a half ago and has no urgency. The only person affected by the timing on this is me and I am asking for a week's break so I have time to contact my family myself,' I wrote.

Now, rather than meeting on more or less equal footing, I was starting off on the back foot, and instead of carefully crafting a podcast and recording my research, I was in a race with a tabloid newspaper to find my brothers and at least let them know that dear old dad was about to hit the headlines again, in an attempt to mitigate, if not control, the message. And while I had grown up in White Plains ignorant of our shared history, they had lived with the real-life fallout of their father's fall from grace. My considered approach was replaced by a desperate urgency.

Using the information that Isabel provided, I looked up the Brodie brothers on Facebook. My eldest brother had posted some pictures of himself from when he was a young man in his early twenties, with a beard and long hair.

'Hey, Dexter, look at this: it's me with a beard!' We gazed at our own eyes smiling back at us.

We were peeping through the keyhole at our family like spies. We were an off-shoot, a rogue spur off the family tree, a branch line. And a story that felt like my story alone, was suddenly about Dexter too.

But Dexter doesn't feel the illegitimacy as I do; he has always looked like his family and he resembles this family too. To me our features felt borrowed without permission, stolen. The feeling of being on the outside looking in was reignited in me and I was the bastard who stole the Brodie eyes. Part of my inheritance from my birth father is a legacy of coveting what wasn't ours, even my genes were stolen goods.

Even so, I hurried to leave voice messages for my brothers on all the numbers I had. I wrote to them on Facebook. 'My name is Donna Freed and Mira Lindenmaier is my mother and Alvin Brodie was my father. I think I'm your half sister.' I spelled out my full name and email address and phone numbers so that they could look me up on social media.

Isabel asked me if Mira would speak on the record and if she could be in touch with her. I knew the answer to both of those questions, but I dutifully provided her with the lawyer's name and number knowing full well that it would take a miracle for him to get back to her. Predictably, he didn't.

Isabel informed me that the story was going to press on October 20, Simon's birthday. She repeated that she needed to speak with Mira. She may not have had the assistance of my band of amateur sleuths, but she was an actual investigative reporter. If she wanted to speak to Mira, she could track her down. It wasn't my job to turn Mira in.

Of course, what very much was my responsibility was to call Mira myself. I had to forewarn her that her life was due, once again to be splashed across the Sunday paper and that it was me who had thoughtlessly spilled the beans. What had I done? I had crossed a line and risked jeopardising our relationship with this idiotic stunt. I felt like Arlene Pralle who adopted serial killer Aileen Wuornos, only to sell her story.

I was shaking as I held the phone waiting for her to pick up just as I was when I called her the very first time. On this occasion, I knew what was at stake and I did not want to lose Mira.

'I have some news that you're not going to like,' I told her. 'Oh?'

'I'm so sorry,' I finished my shaky confession in a whisper.

'Well,' she said, 'at least it's not the *New York Times*. It could be worse.'

I blubbered my thankful relief. The fear of rejection was still close to the surface and our connection, when tested, felt tenuous.

After all that, the story got bumped again but finally featured in the November 3 edition.

Fortuitously, 'You found your brother!' came through on WhatsApp a week earlier on October 27. It was from my brother's wife, Grace – my half sister-in-law? 'It's your big brother, Tony' he said when I called. After the initial joyous rush of catching up that I had experienced with Mira, he told me about our father. 'When *Catch Me if You Can* came out, we thought it was about Dad!' In the 2002 film Leonardo DiCaprio plays chameleon-like conman Frank Abagnale. By the time the article came out, I had also spoken to Frank and Billy, the second and third oldest. They all acknowledged that Alvin and Mira's stunt and particularly Alvin going to prison plunged their family into penury. 'We had to go on welfare,' Tony recalled. But there was not a trace of resentment or malice towards me. I recorded nothing. I simply lapped up their voices and their welcome.

They shared their stories, sometimes brutal, of Alvin as a father. As a man, though, they seemed to have an enduring if somewhat begrudging respect for his constant scheming. The tales of neglect and violence at Alvin's hands were variations on a theme, as were the stories of his scams. He forged traveller's checks, treated them to plane tickets to Puerto Rico that he didn't pay for and weren't in their own names, he was a no-show at a graduation because he was arrested at the airport. He once asked Billy to pretend they were brothers, not father and son, to appear younger to his lover. The lover was hit with a double whammy when his age was revealed by the arresting officers in yet another failed venture. The cheque Alvin wrote Billy and his wife for their wedding bounced, 'insufficient funds'. He was known to favour a white suit and proffer his ring to be kissed. He sounded a good deal better from this distance, I was glad I was meeting the newer and improved version of him in his sons. They were charming and cheeky, quick-witted and funny. Most of all they were welcoming and I felt embraced and grateful. Billy and his family recorded a beautiful Thanksgiving greeting that reduced me to tears.

Tony and Grace remembered meeting Mira. 'She was around after Dad got out of jail.' When Alvin left the House of Detention for Men, he seemed to pick up right where he left off, moving back to the family home and keeping Mira on the side. He and Louise had another child, so I have four half-brothers and a half-sister.

They each in their own way were scarred by Alvin. They knew his most reliable traits were his vanity and hubris but they also seemed open to what he could and did offer them, flawed as he was. They were also far more responsible parents themselves, to the point of proud and doting.

I met Frank in the afternoon after I landed in New York. On my way in the cab, I worried we wouldn't recognise each other, but as soon as I was out of the car I could see him and was pulled into a big bear hug.

On our way to lunch, we stopped at the various boutique hotels and clubs which his nursery supplied with plants. We discovered that our work and clients had overlapped when I had worked in interior design in the same neighbourhood. Over chicken salad, Frank assured me that I wouldn't have had an overly warm reception from Alvin. 'If you had met him he would have asked you for money, no question.'

'So there's six of us. Do you think I'm the only other one?' I asked Frank. We both laughed. 'Who knows,' he said, 'but it's funny you ask. His last girlfriend had a daughter, and she was young when they got together and Alvin was actually a really good dad to her.'

When Al died, none of the siblings wanted his ashes except Frank. It wasn't sentimentality about Alvin, more the idea that their father should be claimed as well as a sense of history. But then Lauren, the daughter of Alvin's partner, called the brothers, crying and begging to have Alvin's ashes. 'He was a father to me,' she said and so Frank handed them over.

Frank presented me with all of Alvin's writing that he had saved. Among the pile of papers was a short story, 'Fawn and Felix' by Thegn Balencorte about two squirrels who help each other's families during a 'brutal winter.' The longest story, of a more autobiographical nature, is 'Abandon Plan A' by Al Brodie. The main character is Thane Stuart and concerns a failed heist. It opens with the line: 'It was my first arrest, I was thirty-five, in love with Linda, married to Louise and going with Tonya and others ...'

The next morning, I flew to Fort Lauderdale and after spending the day with Mira, I drove to Tony and Grace's where they had invited me to stay the night. They met on Long Island, where Alvin's mother (my grandmother!) lived, around the time Alvin got out of prison, so Grace was familiar with the history. They continued a story Frank had started the previous day. Frank had been mistaken for someone else in their rough, mostly Irish, Manhattan neighbourhood and was stabbed and nearly died. In reaction, Alvin packed his wife and children off to live in California near her parents. Tony didn't go as he had already met Grace and started working. It was around this time that they remembered meeting Mira in Alvin's company.

Tony and Grace took me out to a buzzing Italian restaurant, where they seemed to know everyone. Their daughter and her husband met us there. I had the feeling that along with her genuine curiosity about me, she was also protective of her parents and their open and loving natures. They are an affectionate family and I was overwhelmed by their generosity and warmth.

I flew back to New York and on January 7, 2020 I appeared on the *Today Show* as part of their 'Secrets' series. They had contacted me after the *New York Post* article was published. It was a short spot about finding my story and then finding Mira.

Mira was tickled for me and astonished that Tony and Grace remembered her let alone had expressed an interest in visiting her. She didn't seem at all concerned that expanding my birth family circle beyond her might reduce her role in my life.

And then the world seemed to stop spinning. By March 7, Mira's nursing home had closed its doors to visitors and restricted residents to their rooms. On April 20, Julie emailed me to say that the local Florida paper reported cases of Covid-19 at the facility.

It was harder than ever to get through to Mira. With the residents confined to their rooms, the nurses and aides were forced to attend to each of them individually, moving slowly from room to room. When I did get through, they asked me to call back in ten minutes, thirty minutes or an hour. In early May, after a full week of failed attempts, the residents were assigned direct numbers.

We were all living in the elastic and intangible dimension of repetitive loops like the 'Ground Hog' day that Mira had repeated for untold years – I still didn't know how long exactly, but my best guess was a decade. Each day the same and always with the TV on. Mira's direct line rang and rang.

'Hi Donna! I'm your cousin!:)' was the email's subject line. Another Alvin connection, I assumed, there must be dozens.

But the email was from Mira's niece; the elusive North Carolina cousin who I had been trying to find. She had seen the *Today Show* footage and recognised who I must be. Her name is Jeanine.

I had been barking up the wrong family tree. I had been looking for a Maria to no avail. Mira had called her Masha or Maryasha, Russian nicknames for Maria. 'She's a scientist,' Mira had told me. 'She's divorced and has two daughters. My sister and her son also live in the area.' The most I had been able to find was Mira's sister listed among her college's alumni. When Seymour died, I cast aside any hope of finding Mira's relatives, as I no longer had any compelling reason to visit Chapel Hill. I assumed they would become aware of me in some fashion in the event of Mira's death and left it at that.

But here was my cousin Jeanine and we had lockdown hours aplenty to while away on WhatsApp. I was eager to relay all the information Mira had passed on. 'I've been trying to find you!' She confirmed everything Mira had said and told me that she had been looking for me for years. As an indication of how overwhelmed I was by the surprise of meeting her, it only belatedly dawned on me to ask, 'Wait, why were *you* looking for me? How did you know about me?'

Jeanine is a scientist, energetic, upbeat and naturally very curious. Her grandmother – and mine – died in 1998, the same year that Google launched their search engine. Jeanine asked herself, what could possibly come up using her grandmother's singular name in a search? The internet hadn't even existed for most of Braina Lindenmaier's lifetime.

Jeanine's screen filled with the identical rows of articles as mine had and she had scrolled through and read them with a thirst that matched my own. But unlike me, these were faces she recognised; these were people she knew, her people, her family. Her pregnant aunt, flanked by her grandparents, descended the courthouse steps and that baby who was given up for adoption, that was her cousin. 'I thought I came from a boring family but now it was like a soap opera!'

As it happened, her family was not too dissimilar to mine when it came to secrets. She told her brother, but not their mother. She also did not mention it to her aunt, Mira. 'I felt that if they hadn't said anything about it, they didn't want me to know about it.' Keep the cat inside the bag at all times!

She was excited by the idea an unknown cousin but had no way to find me until her brother sent her the clip of me on the *Today Show*. She was mystified when it arrived sans explanation but it became apparent as soon as she saw me and heard my story. And then she put my name into a google search and found me through *Radio Gorgeous*.

Jeanine grew up spending weekends at the home of her grandmother, who had changed her name to Bronja. Her grandfather, Werner, who Anne of Spence-Chapin had said was 'quiet and withdrew into his work to cope with his stress' had passed away before Jeanine was born. When she spoke about our grandmother, I almost had the impulse to correct her, so strong was the image of Braina that I had created in my mind from the fragments in those distant articles and extra details Mira had added over the years. I was so accustomed to living off the crumbs of stories that there was hardly room for tangible reality.

But as I listened to Jeanine, I did recognise her Aunt Mira, the mother that I had come to know. 'She was different,' Jeanine said, 'reserved, a bit aloof.' How could Jeanine have known that her very existence, a beloved granddaughter in the house, was likely an affront to Mira, a symbol of all that she had lost.

Jeanine also confirmed the impression I had formed, that until her move to Florida, Mira had remained arrested in her development, resentful of her mother's meddling in her adult life, cleaning up what she – and the police and media – perceived as Mira's mess. While Braina thought she had helped Mira make good her escape and was acting in her best interest, Mira only saw that her mother was making all the decisions for her. She went behind her mother's back like a rebellious teenager to continue seeing the man who had brought shame to their door, who had brought Mira so low. 'She was mad when she found out I was still seeing him' she had told me.

I didn't tell Mira at first that I was in touch with Jeanine. It didn't feel like betrayal exactly, more like losing ownership of her own family narrative. I hadn't gone behind her back or conspired with Jeanine, but it also didn't feel quite straightforward.

I heard the disappointment in Jeanine's voice when I told her that I wasn't going to tell Mira that we were in touch just yet, but then again, she wasn't planning to tell her mother either. I had every intention of telling Mira, but I wanted to wait until the sting of the *New York Post* and *Today Show* faded a little. I might be able to tell her in person when this plague lifted.

Instead, I sent her pictures of Dexter and our new puppy, Ruby. They were our only news, but it was adorable news that was a most welcome distraction from the sluggish monotony of lockdown.

Like everyone else, we had cancelled our holiday abroad and instead arranged to stay in the medieval town of Rye in East Sussex for a change of routine and scenery. I didn't get through to Mira before we left but resolved to call her as soon as we were back.

On the afternoon of Monday, August 3, after a day at the beach chasing an exuberant Ruby in the sunshine at Camber Sands, I checked my email. 'Please call Memorial Hospital NOW!' It was from Julie. 'Donna, I just received a call from Ruth at Memorial Hospital. She asked you to contact her right away. Ruth wouldn't tell me anything, other than that Mira is in the ICU.'

Ruth explained that Mira had been admitted to the hospital with breathing difficulties. 'Your mother doesn't have Covid,' she said, which was initially reassuring until her next words, which were even more chilling. Mira had calcifications around her right lung that were making it impossible for her to breathe and she also had a hernia on the left lung. 'Was she exposed to asbestos at some point in her life?' Ruth wanted to know. Mira had been intubated and they had tried unsuccessfully to wean her off the ventilator; she could not breathe on her own. Although Mira was not sedated, she was not responsive either. Her condition was 'not reversible'. The sole course of treatment available was to perform a tracheotomy and insert a feeding tube.

'Do you know if your mother has a Living Will or a Do Not Resuscitate order? Would she want a tracheotomy or a feeding tube?' Ruth asked.

When I told her that my mother's name was also Ruth,

it helped explain that while Mira was my mother, I hadn't known her long and why I might not know if Mira had been exposed to asbestos. 'She was a smoker at some point,' was the most I could offer. I didn't know if she wanted a tracheotomy or a feeding tube any more than I knew any of her medical history or if she had a middle name.

'I called the lawyer on file but he said he doesn't work for your mother any longer.'

I told Ruth that I was in touch with my cousin and that we should be able to find out if Mira's sister had any paperwork.

'In the meantime, I can put you through to your mother so you can talk to her.'

A nurse placed the phone by Mira's head. I stood in the kitchen of a building that dates back to the 1500s but also has a barrel-vaulted Norman cellar. It was part of the Flushing Inn whose infamous former landlord was the murderous butcher John Breads, the last man to be hanged in Rye for the stabbing of Allen Greball in 1743 in the churchyard across the cobbled way. Breads' skull sits in the attic of the Town Hall. I looked out of the window whose sill is over a foot thick and spoke to my mother whose voice I first heard eight years ago and who was three thousand miles away in Florida. I told her that I was in touch with Jeanine. I told her how much I loved her and that I felt blessed to have found her. I told her that I was looking at my thumbs and that I was sorry. I told her I wished I was there to hold her. I told her she was safe, that I was holding her in my heart, in my clenched fist. I had no idea if she could hear me.

Jeanine called the lawyer anyway and to my surprise, he admitted that he did have paperwork. He said, 'I didn't say anything when the hospital called because I wasn't paid for the last five years.'

There were two documents attached to his email. The first was a Florida Durable Power of Attorney with Respect to

Health Care of the Person and Designation of Health Care Surrogate and the second was a Declaration under Life-Prolonging Procedures Act of Florida.

In the first, Miriam Lindenmaier appointed Donna Freed as her Attorney-in-Fact and 'Health Care Surrogate.' In the event that it became necessary to appoint a guardian of her person, Miriam Lindenmaier nominated her 'biological daughter Donna Freed', as such guardian.

In the second, Mira stated her wish that life-prolonging measures be withheld or withdrawn should her attending or treating physician determine that there was no medical probability of recovery and that the life-prolonging procedures would serve only to artificially prolong the process of dying. In the absence of her own ability to give directions regarding the application of life-prolonging procedures, she designated Donna Freed to carry out the provisions of her Declaration.

Both documents were signed and witnessed on 10 October 2013 and listed her former address on 20th Avenue in Hollywood as her residence.

Despite Covid-19 raging throughout South Florida, the doctor was patient with me. He answered my questions thoroughly and calmly. He confirmed that the words in the document, 'terminal', 'end-stage', 'persistent', and 'prolong artificially' all now applied to Mira and barred him from administering a tracheotomy or feeding tube. It was also a clear mandate to remove the ventilator.

He remained equally understanding when I told him that I could not start the countdown clock while tripping over the cobbles of ancient Rye overseen by the ghost of a murderous landlord. I needed to be in my own home for that. I had to hold the shell of her cockle heart, to end the life of the mother who so dramatically gave me mine. Her other gift, this terrible duty.

While we drove back to London, the nurses propped up

the phone for Mira's sister to say her farewells and again for Julie to say her goodbyes and prayers.

At home, I sat on my bed, where I had often spoken with Mira and called the doctor. I confirmed that I believed that I was fulfilling Mira's wishes to remove life support and administer only such palliative care that would make her more comfortable. They sent me a link for a video call in Mira's room. As soon as someone became available, they would activate the camera at her end. I waited in the kitchen, standing at attention by the laptop on the counter.

When the camera clicked on, it felt eerily like a hostage video. She was so far away and from this remove I could offer no comfort, only deliver the coup de grace. Simon and Dexter held me from behind, their arms tethering me. I said 'Thank you' and 'I love you' and 'Goodbye, Mama Mira'. Over and over again.

The phone rang after 2 a.m. The hospice nurse had arrived. She would meet with the doctors but it was shift change time, she would call again once the extubation had taken place. I held Mira in my heart and my hands.

'It's done. I'm not sure how long it will take, but I will call you when she has passed.'

Almost a day later, the nurse called for the final time.

I informed the lawyer and he sent Mira's Last Will and Testament also dated 10 October, 2013. Under immediate family, there is one name: 'my biological daughter, Donna Freed'.

I didn't grieve for Mira in the same way as I had for Ruth. She didn't live in my bones the way Ruth did. Though Ruth never heard about or visited our house in London, she is integral to it. I still feel her everywhere. I carry Mira with me but not in me. But I was similarly destabilised by her passing. The current of her death rippled through me and I bobbled

240

like a cork in her wake. All the more so because this time, I really was without parents.

I didn't take in the reality of Mira's passing as I had done with Ruth's or my father's. In the past, I had been sealed off from the normal hurly-burly of life, glassed inside a bubble of mourning. I could notice and mark the waning of my grief when I was able to step back into the swing of things and resume my participation in life. But Mira's death took place in a vacuum. We were all stuck and there was no movement, only lockdown and quarantine and awful 'new normals'. The comparative landscape had been shattered. There was no normal to return to so how could I chart my path back to it?

This mourning was also mine to shoulder alone. There were no siblings to share its burden and other than Simon and Dexter, no one else knew her.

I awoke one morning with the sudden realisation that as Mira's heir, the one thing I had been bequeathed was the keys to our joint past. In January of 2013 I had contacted Anne at Spence-Chapin to ask her if it was possible to get copies of my adoption file now that Mira and I were reunited. 'In answer to your question, sadly, no,' she wrote. 'However, your birth mother is allowed to have back everything she signed ... [we] will assign your birth mother to one of our Interns, who will request a notarized letter from your mother, and then will release her original signed documents back to her.'

I didn't want to ask Mira to do all that and nor did I think she would jump through the required hoops. Little did I know, she was leaping through similar legal hoops of her own nine months later.

When I asked Spence-Chapin about the records and Anne's email after Mira's death, the answer was unequivocal: 'In New York, adoption records are sealed under the law, and therefore Spence-Chapin is legally unauthorized to release the record. If your birth mother was still with us, she too would be ineligible to receive the record ... I cannot speak to the actions of former employees, but I can speak to our current policies, which are governed by New York law: the documents signed by birth parents are part of the sealed adoption record and cannot be released as per NY Domestic Relations Law Section 114.'

Mira had written away her rights to her own words and they could not be reclaimed by her or anyone else; those skeletons would be buried with hers.

I don't know why Mira didn't tell me that she had actually changed her will and Power of Attorney, only that she intended to. It had obviously been a tremendous effort to do so. She had to ask someone to call the lawyer and then instruct him in the changes, approve them and then sign the paperwork. She did all that and didn't tell me. It is impossible to believe that she accomplished all of that, the stuff of daily life for some but not for her, and then forgot. Maybe she worried I would view it as an imposition, or she wanted to see if I would stick around without that obligation, or maybe the words grew too big to say.

Secrets are almost always exposed but not always in time to do any good.

In the mail I received back the photo album and the replacement heart cockle shell I had brought for Mira on my last visit. I put her cockle heart with mine, in a silver box engraved with my uncle's initials. They lie together with my father's wedding ring, one of Dexter's baby teeth and Ruth's hand-written speech from our wedding, ' . . .you will find an even richer, deeper love . . .'

Epilogue

A FINAL TWIST IN THE TALE

As her internal battle cleared, Ruth found the courage to change her behaviour and the vantage point from which she viewed her children; like a fever passing, she saw us afresh. She was able to regard us without suspicion, full of positive faith. She became compassionate, encouraging and helpful. In these changes were writ an unspoken acknowledgement of all that had passed before. If it weren't broke, she wouldn't have fixed it and, for me, the fixing provided us both with the redemption we so desired. I drank in those changes in her as the mother's milk that belatedly nourished me. We grew as vines, tightly wrapped around each other, our curling tendrils reaching round.

In the end, my relationship with Ruth looked like a rather ordinary, mother-daughter relationship. Ruth was a mother who was happy for her daughter to be married, excited about becoming a grandmother again and supportive when I gave birth. I was a daughter who looked to her mother for advice and was distraught when she became ill and devastated when she died. It doesn't sound like the stuff of miracles, but it was miles from where we started and that was plenty miraculous for me.

Mira and I were pre-disposed to love each other, and our relationship grew quickly in trust and confidence. But our foundation wasn't deeply rooted in a shared history or habit, we only had the bond of a mother to an unborn child and one fraught first week of life to draw upon. Circumstances, distance, time and especially, the nature of our parting, all worked against us, but I know both our lives were made richer by our reunion.

My mothers pool in me; one my earth, the other my water. Perhaps what Mira instilled in me prepared me for Ruth and what Ruth drew out of me readied me for Mira. I came to them both with an open heart. I was destined to be a fool for my mothers' love.

Whatever is in my power to forgive, I forgive. There are many factors that lead me to forgiveness: one is choice, another is the acceptance that comes with age, and another is gratitude, but also because I too, wish to be forgiven.

The downward pressure of trauma – my mothers' compiled within me and compounded by my own – and learned behaviour grinds heavily through our generations. I am hopeful that the intensity of that pressure, however inescapable, is lessening as we pass it along our family chain from mother and mother to daughter to son.

When I first read Spence-Chapin's background report and the newspaper articles I thought I was the reason for my parents' ill-fated folly, that I was the embryo of the story and in the story. But no, that was Mira and Alvin's story alone. I merely had a walk-on part in the final scene.

Mira was pregnant when she faked her death, but it was a matter of days, possibly weeks at most. She may have recognised the tell-tale signs from her earlier, terminated pregnancies and she very well may not have. She was categorically not pregnant thirty-nine days earlier when she changed the beneficiary of her insurance policies from Werner to Alvin, which was the first step in a plan they had already hatched. I was not part of that plan. If she hadn't been in hiding out in White Plains, she might well have caught a flight back to Puerto Rico.

Did Alvin know and this escalated the pace of their scheme? I tend to doubt it. When the pregnancy became clear to Mira, it must have added to her fears. Alvin claimed the insurance money in September and yet she didn't hear from him. By the end of November, she would have been in no doubt about being pregnant. Was that what she wanted to tell him when she called on Thanksgiving Day?

And so, I was not the turning of the tide that caused the cascade. That was not my story.

That was just the beginning of a great story that started with them and took all its twists and turns and turned into me. It's all my story, I'll take all of it and I give it all to you, Dexter.

Acknowledgements

To my brother and sister who lit the way: you were there throughout and I am deeply glad that you still are.

Thank you to my agent, Katie Fulford; we believed in each other from the outset and you brought me to Muswell Press which felt like coming home to the dream team that is Kate and Sarah Beal and all the phenomenal writers they have fostered.

I owe a debt of gratitude to the documentary film-maker and tenacious blood-hound for the facts, Lisa Stevens for her research and enthusiasm. Also to Josephine Pembroke, to whom I am so happy I said yes! And to our Radio Gorgeous family, who taught me that success is doing and demonstrate it every day. Thank you, Jo Rees, for your unstinting generosity and for showering the world with joy wherever you go.

Thank you to *The Oldie* and Isabel Vincent at the *New York Post* for publishing articles on my story.

To Julia Ragona, for all that you are and all that you have ever been. To my other early readers, Jennifer Ladonne, Orna Klement, Kate, McKamy, Penny Philips and Greg Sanders, I so appreciate your time and thoughtful comments. Your encouragement was invaluable; your friendship even more so. My grateful thanks also to Fiona Brownlee and Laura Mcfarlane of Muswell Press.

Peter Laguerre, Jeffrey Donaldson-Forbes and Marcus

Berardino, do away with the word adoption and it's still true: you are my angels. Thank you Douglas Johnston for never taking me too seriously or allowing me to do so.

To my most precious Dexter, you are the most delightful astonishment. I am desperately proud of you but can take none of the credit, you do all the work.

And finally, thank you to Simon, for guiding me to that deeper love that is a marriage. You are an endless pool of support and laughter, and you, my love, were the essential turning of my life's tide.